Copyright ©2025, The Fontaine Collection
ALL RIGHTS RESERVED.

No part of this publication may be reproduced, stored in a retrieval system, or transmitted in any form or by any means—electronic, mechanical, photocopy, recording, or any other—except for brief quotation in reviews, without the prior permission of the author or publisher.

Second Edition August 2025

ISBN: 978-1-962402-09-5

Foreword photography images courtesy of and with permission from Chris O'Dell
Photography by Michelle Pemberton, and Tom and Mary Fontaine and Fontaine archives

All the memorabilia items, documents, etc. pictured in this book were previously owned by collector Tom Fontaine
Book layout and design by Tom Fontaine and Robin Surface

FOREWORD

When I was born in Muncie, Indiana, little could I have imagined that I would work for The Beatles in London or the Rolling Stones, and Bob Dylan, and that George Harrison would write a song about me. In Indianapolis, 63 miles from Muncie, a six year old boy would become the largest Beatles collector of our time. Our paths have now crossed.

Thomas continued through his life to take possession and care for many artifacts from the early days and throughout Beatle history. When speaking to him, I was taken by the love he exudes as he speaks of the many pieces that have come into his care and the sadness when he alludes to the many pieces with which he has parted.

This book may be his last and it certainly may be his best ever. It contains so much of what really represented The Beatles as a group and individually throughout their careers. Looking through the book, I felt as though I was looking at someone's children's photos! That's how much they mean to him.

I am so happy to have been introduced to Tom and to have the opportunity to see what he has made his life's purpose.

It gives me great pleasure to introduce you to (unless you are already acquainted with) Thomas Fontaine.

Chris O'Dell
March 2023

Chris O'Dell and George Harrison

Above, single, "Miss O'Dell", written by George Harrison. Right, Chris (far right) along with (left to right) Yoko Ono, Maureen Starkey and Ken Mansfield at The Beatles' last concert appearance on the rooftop at Apple Records, 3 Savile Row, on January 30, 1969.

INTRODUCTION FROM THE AUTHOR

Welcome to Rare Lifetime Collections. When I released my first book, *Rare, The Memorabilia Collection of a Lifetime,* in 2016, I shared a glimpse of The Beatles in the Archive Section of items I once owned.

That inspired me to create *The Beatles and the Solo Years (A Trip Down Memory Lane)* in 2018. I received many great and positive responses to this book, including: "Brings back great memories of the Beatles in a new refreshing way" and "A great autograph study of The Beatles' signatures throughout their careers." This was amazing, since besides showing the items from my collection, I also wanted to educate people about collecting.

I have decided to conclude this trip with The Beatles with this new installment, *The Beatles Looking Back: The Final Trip.* In this book, I share my entire Beatles catalogue as well as the memories associated with that fifty-year span of my life. More than 600 images take readers on a trip through the history of The Beatles as a group and their individual solo careers. These items were like family to me, and I took ultimate care of each and every one of them while they were in my possession.

It was a bittersweet experience putting this book together, since reliving some of these memories created a bit of seller's remorse for me on more than one occasion. Please don't mistake this as me bragging, I was just the proud caretaker of these pieces and did my best to preserve their history.

The Beatles have been a part of my life as a collector, going all the way back to 1964. The Fab 4 have brought me many fond memories, but now that I am 64 I think it's time to close this chapter of my life. Oh, don't think that I'm done collecting — I still have some great Beatle artifacts in my collection — but this is my final printed tribute to the past. It's my gift to you, the Beatles fans old and new, so you will know that each new day is a day of discovery.

Because some of these images were taken in the past, before I ever thought about image resolution and how they would look when they were printed in a book, the quality varies. Many of them were taken for my personal enjoyment and documentation, so I could keep a photographic scrapbook of all the items I collected.

As you enjoy the complete cataloging of my collection, you will encounter items I owned that may look familiar in print and have now found new homes with collectors and fans. I hope you enjoy the way I have presented them.

I did not do this alone. I had many fortunate opportunities to communicate one-on-one with the people who originally obtained these items. They shared their stories with me and I did my very best to preserve their legacy, whether it be an autograph, document, etc. Knowing the stories made the items even more special.

I also have to recognize and thank other collectors, dealers, auction houses, organizations, etc. that gave me the chance to own these items. As life goes on, I have lost contact with many of them, but they know who they are. I do thank you for sharing this part of my journey over the years.

Lastly, this would have never have happened if it was not for the love, support, and patience of my family and dear friends — I am deeply grateful to all of you!!

Dear Readers, I hope you enjoy this book for many years to come.

Tom Fontaine
April 2023

FILMMAKER WEITZMAN'S THOUGHTS ABOUT THE AUTHOR AND 'THE FINAL TRIP'

I've had the privilege of knowing Tom Fontaine and his wonderful wife, Mary, for the best part of five years. Tom is truly the kindest, most knowledgeable, enthusiastic and sensitive person. His vast array of collections, from sports through the arts and entertainment are simply jaw dropping, especially when you think that he started collecting almost sixty years ago at the age of five and came from a very humble family.

As a child, Tom started picking up discarded Beatles picture cards on a rainy summer day in 1964, and that would lead him to his uncle's store where he carried the cards that would begin Tom's lifelong journey as a collector of just about everything. Collecting soon became a passion for him, which in turn formed his career.

Tom is not a traditional collector. He is a preserver and curator of precious artifacts, that in many cases would have otherwise been lost to the world, condemned to obscure history books, or even buried in a landfill. He is a modern-day Indiana Jones, constantly discovering hidden treasures and going deeper into their back stories than anyone else I know.

What I admire so much about Tom is his willingness to share these artifacts and collections in his books, which are full of amazing facts, personal stories and information — none more so than in this current book. His Beatles collection is an Aladdin's cave of wonderment. I don't see what Tom produces as just "books," for me they are published exhibitions that stir the imagination and bring popular history to life for everyone, whoever they are, whatever their age.

As you turn the pages of this book, you will experience the love and passion that Tom poured into this project.

Simon Weitzman
Filmmaker, artist and author

Simon has more than 300 network TV credits to his name, including several involving The Beatles and their world. He has also produced and authored four books on The Beatles: *The Beatles: All You Need Is Love, The Beatles: Tom Murray's Mad Day Out, Eight Arms to Hold You: 50 Years of Help! and the Beatles,* and *The Beatles In Stereographic 3D,* as well as the 2023 film, *A Love Letter to the Beatles — Here, There & Everywhere,* a film celebrating 50+ years of Beatles Fandom.

In addition, he has a background in painting and sculpture, with works exhibited in London, Liverpool and Scotland. Simon also works with people with disabilities to realize their ambitions and unlock their potential.

TABLE OF CONTENTS

The Beatles: Day of Discovery 1

John Lennon 83

Dr. Winston O'Boogie and the Rocket Man 127

Paul McCartney 133

Beatlefest (My Memories) 183

George Harrison 191

Ringo Starr 211

Stuart Sutcliffe (The Forgotten Beatle) 231

The Concert Years, Press Credentials •Advertising • Tickets 239

Posters & Displays 249

Rock 'n' Roll Hall of Fame 261

"The Beatles were in a different stratosphere,
a different planet to the rest of us.
All I know is when I heard 'Love Me Do' on the radio,
I remember walking down the street
and knowing my life was going to be completely different
now the Beatles were in it."

–Justin Hayward, The Moody Blues

THE BEATLES: DAY OF DISCOVERY

In the summer of 1964, while enjoying my vacation from school, a gust of wind changed my life. Summer rains are to be expected in Indianapolis, but on this particular day, the storm came in unusually fast and strong. I ran inside to seek shelter, leaving the back door ajar so I could watch the storm from a safe distance.

Peeking out from the kitchen, I saw my neighbor, Karen Ryza, and her friend running home to avoid the storm. Before the two girls reached the house, the wind blew a bunch of cards out of Karen's hands. Trying to beat the storm, she just kept running and left behind the confetti of cards. A downpour immediately squashed my instinct to run out and see what she'd dropped.

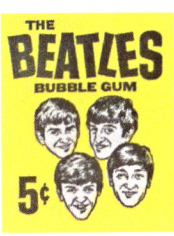

The rain may have delayed my hunt for dropped treasure, but the curious card collector in me couldn't be kept away for long. It took me a few trips to gather the lot because I couldn't stack the cards — they would've stuck together if I did. I couldn't risk ruining the gems I had so patiently waited to retrieve. That would've defeated the purpose.

Upon inspection, I found that each card had a black and white photo on the front and some text on the back. Looking closer, I realized the images were of a four-man band. I honed in on the drumhead detailed on the cards. It read The Beatles. This was my first personal Beatles discovery.

Me and my and Uncle Johnny

I carefully dried the cards, laying them on the air duct register in my room. Once they had dried, I showed them to my mom, who was an early supporter of my collecting tendencies. She said I should go to my Uncle Johnny's grocery store with her that coming Saturday to see if he could identify the cards. Plus, maybe stocked them in his store and I could get more.

I was excited, and my anticipation for Saturday grew throughout the week. When the day finally arrived and we got tot he store, immediately asked, "Uncle Johnny, do you know what these are?"

In a deep, guttural tone he responded, *"Yes. They're those darned Beatles cards."*

"Do you carry them?"

"I have to," he said with a little disgust. *"The girls come in for them all the time."*

And then, without hesitation, my Uncle grabbed five packs of cards and put them in our grocery bag. I could hardly wait to get them home, so I could preserve each wrapper as methodically as the cards inside. After all, the wrappers had images, too, and were an extension of the pack as far as I was concerned.

The highlight of my summer that year became these routine grocery trips with my mother. Each time we visited, Uncle Johnny would casually toss a few packs into our bag.

As time went by and I kept collecting them, there was a different wrapper and the cards inside were printed in color. Despite the change in card design, the thrill of collecting remained the same. I delighted in the ceremonial unveiling of John, Paul, George and Ringo each time I unwrapped a pack. McCord's Drugstore, in my neighborhood, can also be credited with fueling my ever-growing card collection with both baseball and Beatles packs. Thanks to these sources, I amassed quite the collection by the end of that summer.

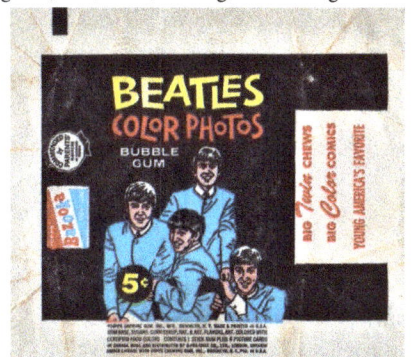

And the rest is history...

"The Beatles first appeared on our show on February 9, 1964, and I have never seen any scenes to compare with the bedlam that was occasioned by their debut.
Broadway was jammed with people for almost eight blocks.
They screamed, yelled, and stopped traffic.
It was indescribable…
There has never been anything like it in show business, and the New York City police were very happy it didn't — and wouldn't— happen again."

— Ed Sullivan
(host of The Ed Sullivan Show)

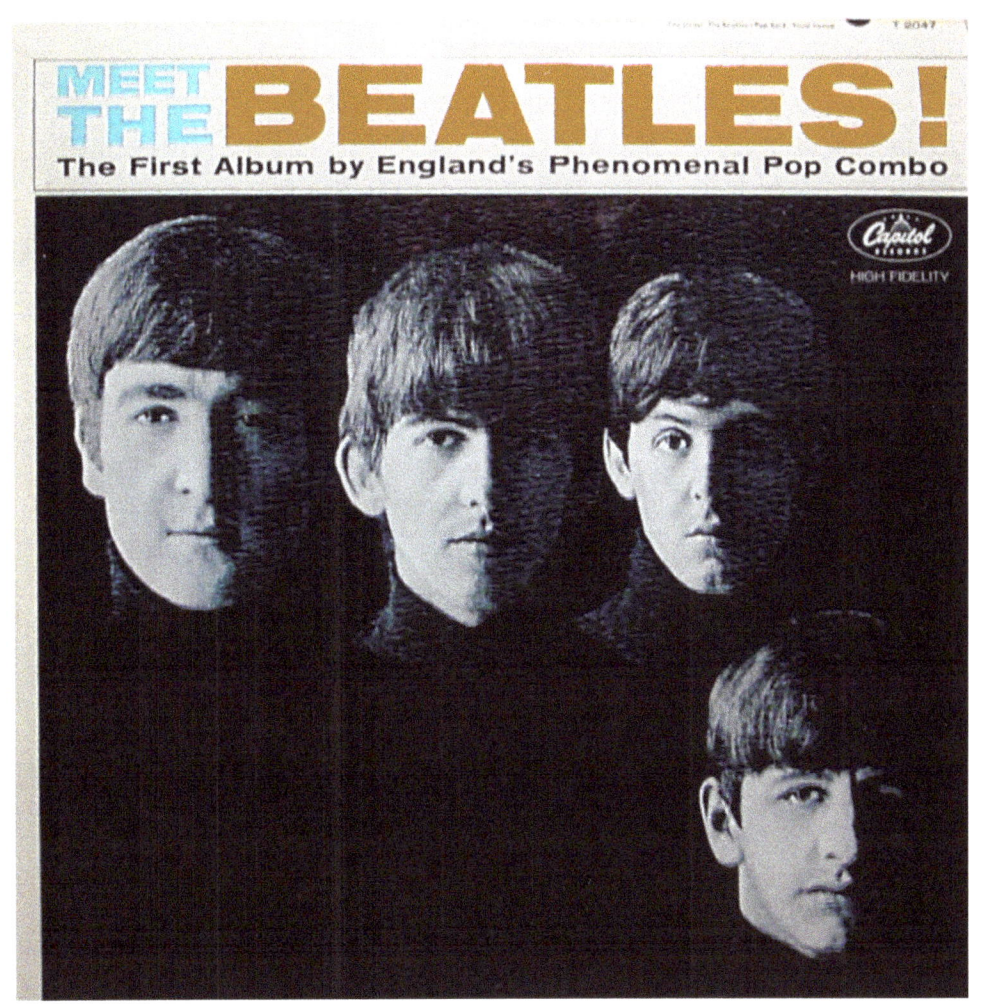

The Beatles

"We were driving through Colorado, we had the radio on,
and eight of the Top 10 songs were Beatles songs…
'I Wanna Hold Your Hand,' all those early ones.
They were doing things nobody was doing.
Their chords were outrageous, just outrageous,
and their harmonies made it all valid…
I knew they were pointing the direction of where music had to go."

— Bob Dylan

Top left, original 6.5 x 4.75 photo of John Lennon with his first band, The Quarrymen. Top right: a rare set of signatures by the original members (minus John), featuring (from left to right as in the picture above) Eric Griffiths, Colin Hanton, Rod Davis, Pete Shotton, and Len Garry.

Above, left and right, Paul McCartney and John Lennon color 11x14 color photographs circa 1960/61. Taken when they were performing at a club during the early period of The Beatles' storied careers. These were printed directly from the original negatives from the Thomas Meenach Archives with his stamp gracing the reverse of the McCartney photograph.

The Beatles Looking Back: The Final Trip

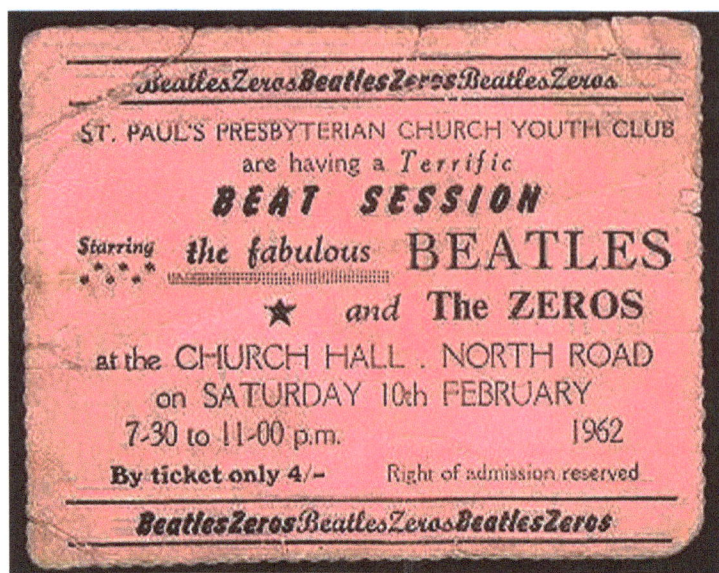

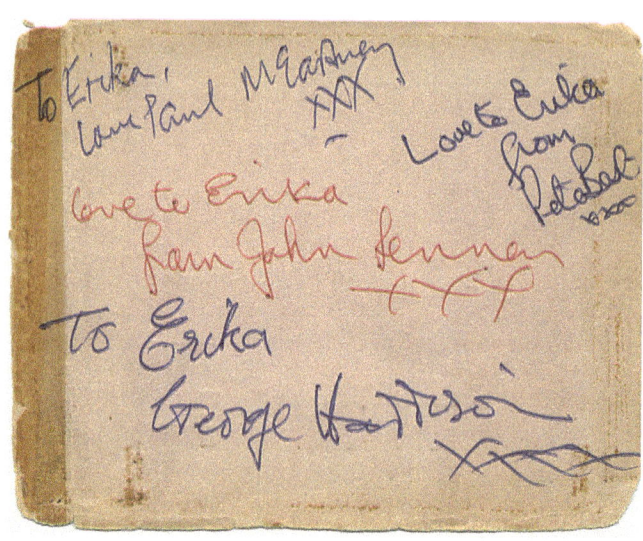

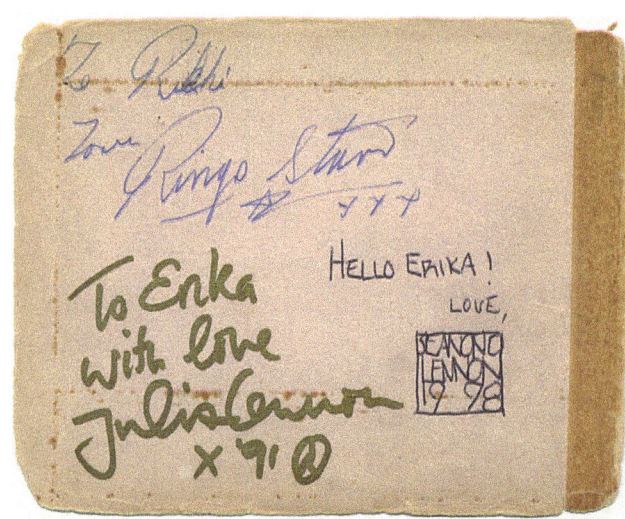

Top and bottom left, very rare signed ticket starring the fabulous Beatles at St Paul's Presbyterian Church Hall Saturday February 10th, 1962.

Top and bottom right, very rare signature ensemble featuring The Beatles with Pate Best, signed at the Cavern Club in early 1962. The reverse is signed by Rory Storm's drummer, Ringo Starr(before joining The Beatles) and later John Lennon's sons, Julian (1991) and Sean in 1998.

The Beatles Looking Back: The Final Trip

An autograph book page signed George, Paul and John from 1962.

A small candid non-Beatle photo signed on the back by The Beatles first drummer, Pete Best.

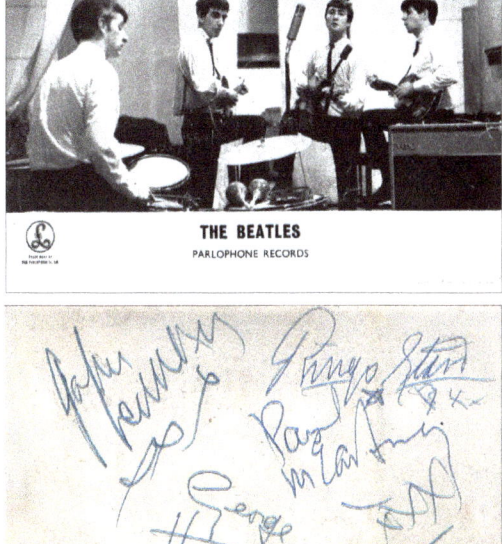

Above, partial Beatles concert ticket from the Majestic Ballroom, signed on the reverse by all four Beatles not to long after Ringo joined the group in August 1962.

Right, Beatles Parlophone card signed in 1962 by all four on the reverse.

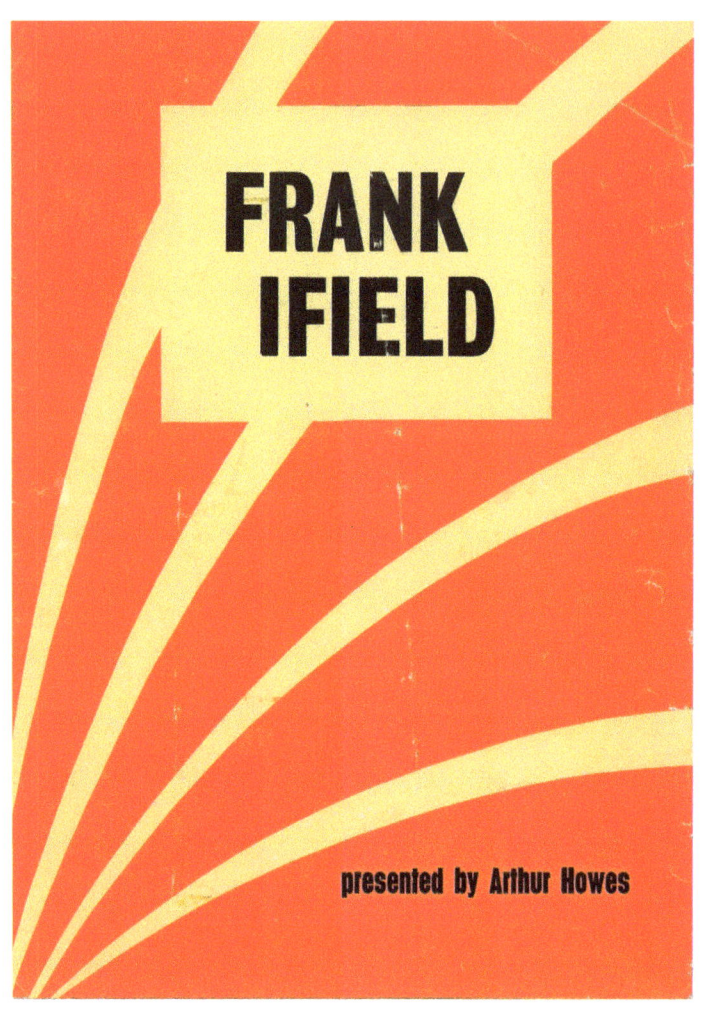

Above is an original autographed program from the December 12, 1962 show at the Embassy Cinema in Peterborough, England. The show featured headliner Frank Ifield and The Beatles. This concert happened due to a phone call from Brian Epstein to Arthur Howes, the country's biggest tour promoter at the time. This one-night-only appearance of The Beatles did not go well, because the Liverpool lads were still somewhat unknown and their music did not appeal to the Frank Ifield ("I'll Remember You") crowd. This program is super rare. I was fortunate enough to purchase it at the Liverpool convention more than 25 years ago. The only image I made of the signatures was a photocopy before it left me to go another collector, but I felt I had to highlight this as one of the best Beatles-signed programs I ever owned.

The Beatles Looking Back: The Final Trip

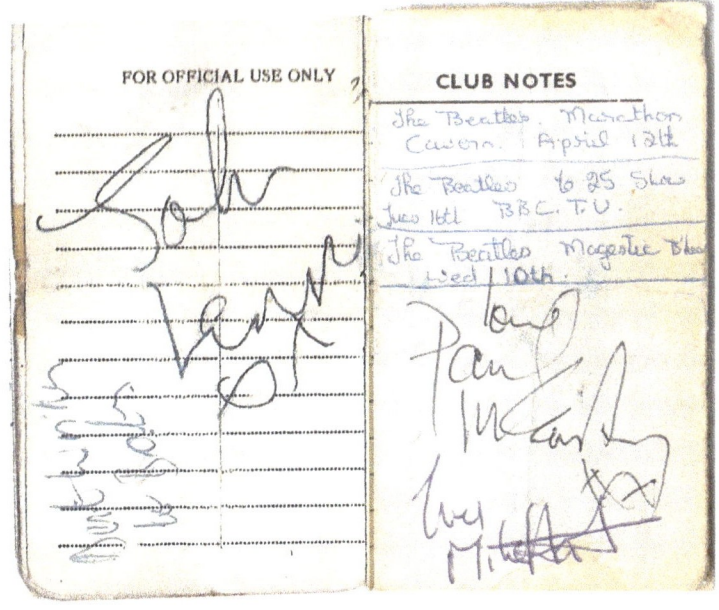
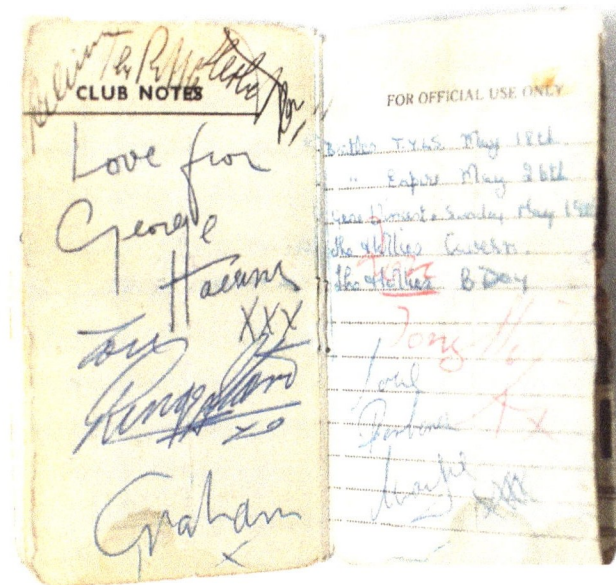

Original 1963 Cavern Club membership book autographed inside by all four Beatles and additionally by the group, The Hollies, including Graham Nash.

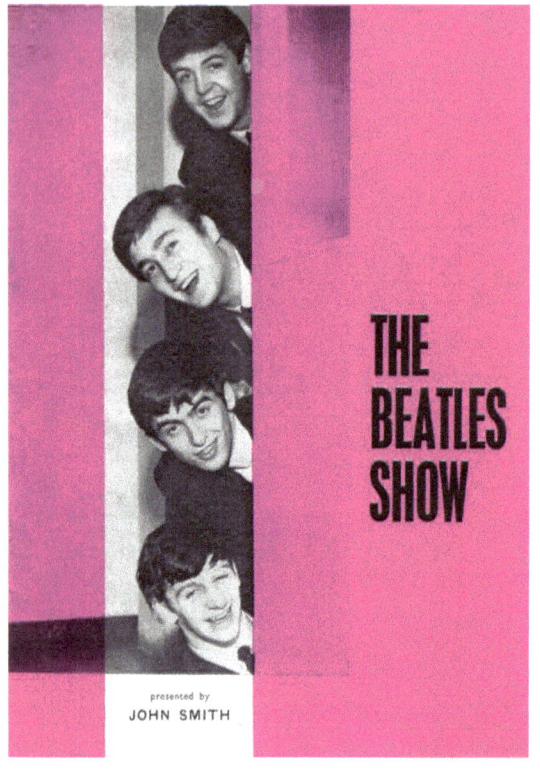

The Beatles Show Program signed by all four Beatles — Incredible!

A Beatles fan's autograph book signed nicely by all four on the first 2 pages. The signatures were obtained in early 1963 and are the only signatures in the book.

The Beatles Looking Back: The Final Trip

The British television show, Thank Your Lucky Stars, original hand-painted camera card used for the opening of the show. The card is autographed and dedicated by all four Beatles. This is the only item to surface from this particular appearance in 1963, as the film was lost and to this day has never surfaced.

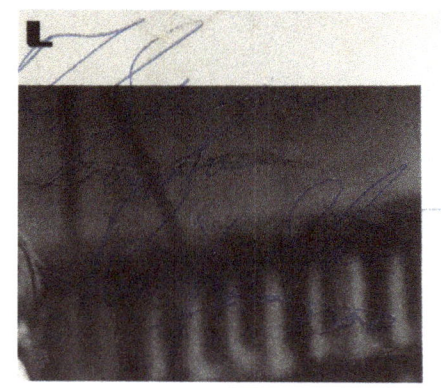

This 1963 English poster is 17.25 x 22 and was purchased at a concert. It was signed by all four Beatles after the show, inscribed to Sue/Susan by Paul, George and Ringo. However, for some reason, John has signed "To Jane". I'm not sure why, but it's Lennon!

The Beatles Looking Back: The Final Trip

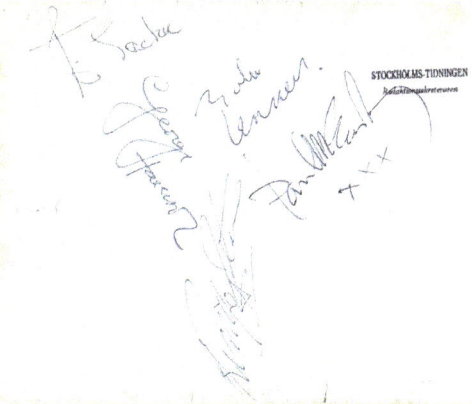

Top left, Please Please Me *UK album cover signed on the reverse by all four Beatles, along with a letter of its history.*

Promotional oversized photo card featuring The Beatles, with signatures by all four on the reverse. Obtained in Sweden, October 1963.

Above, The Beatles concert ticket for Grosvenor signed on the reverse by all four Beatles on May 17, 1963.

The Beatles Looking Back: The Final Trip

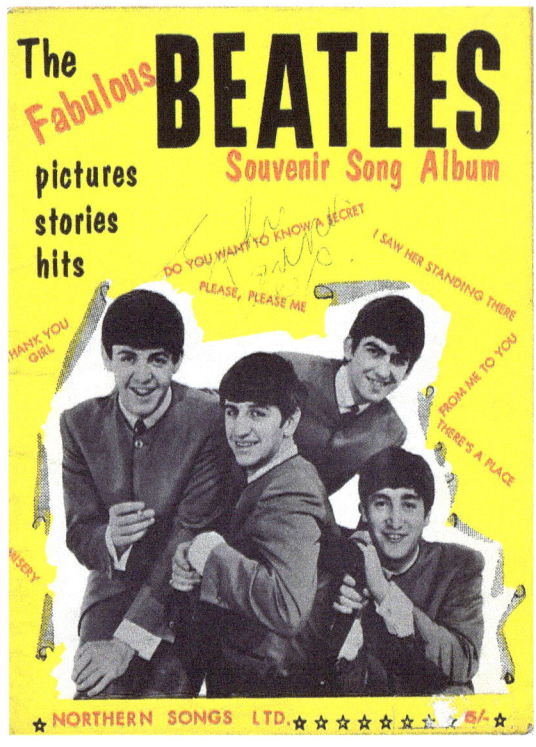

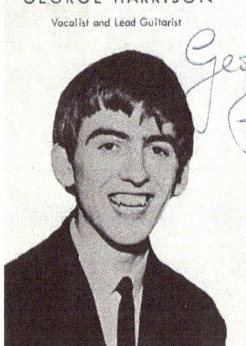

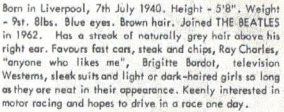

Top right, The Beatles Souvenir Song Album booklet signed by John on the front, and signed by Paul, George, and Ringo on their respective bio pages inside.

Bottom left, A nice Dezo Hoffman photo of the band performing, signed by all four Beatles.

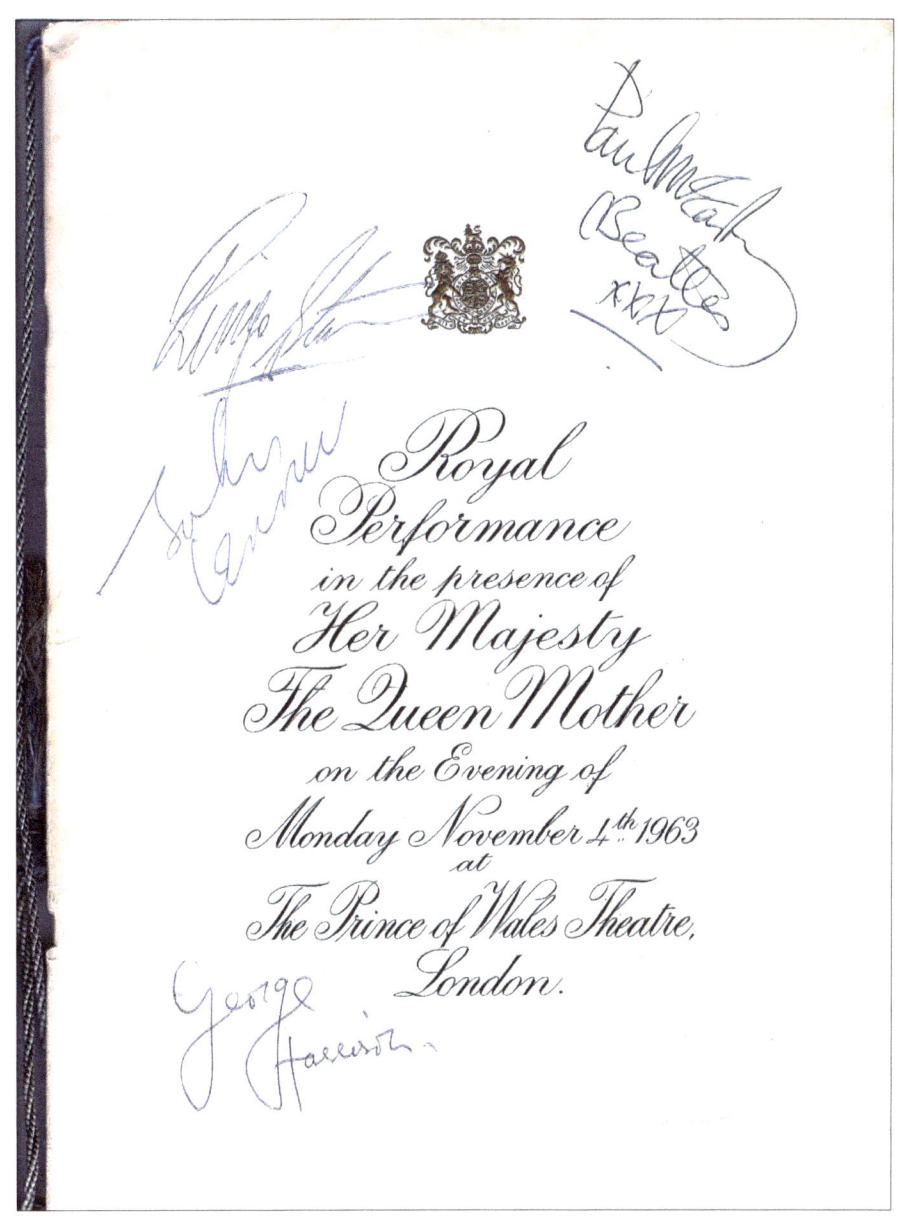

A Royal Command Performance for the Queen Mother *program, signed by all four Beatles on the front cover. This was the performance when John made the famous remark, "Will the people in the cheaper seats clap your hands and the rest of you just rattle your jewelry?"*

The Beatles Looking Back: The Final Trip

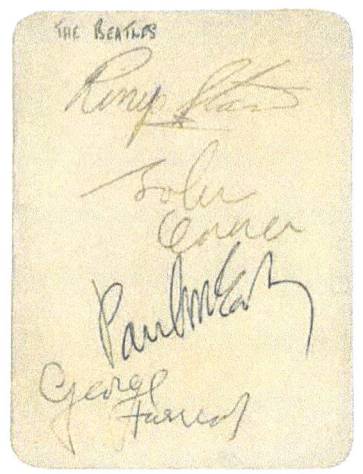

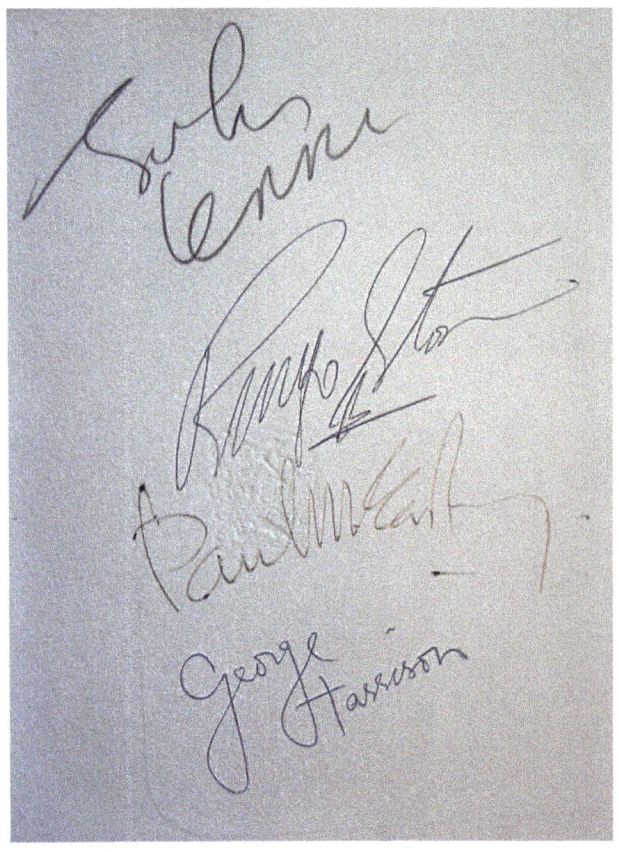

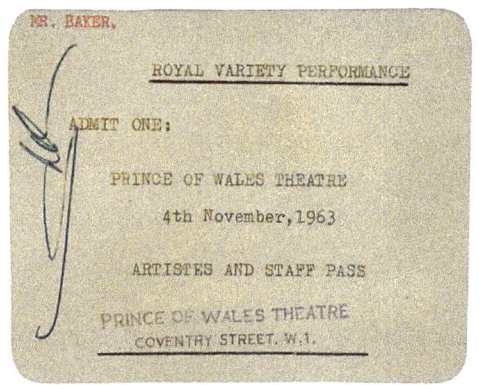

Above, Royal Variety Performance invitation ticket signed by guest performer, Marlene Dietrich who also was a guest performer, plus it's signed by all four Beatles on the reverse.

Left, a Royal Command Performance for the Queen Mother program signed by all four Beatles on the inside of the front cover.

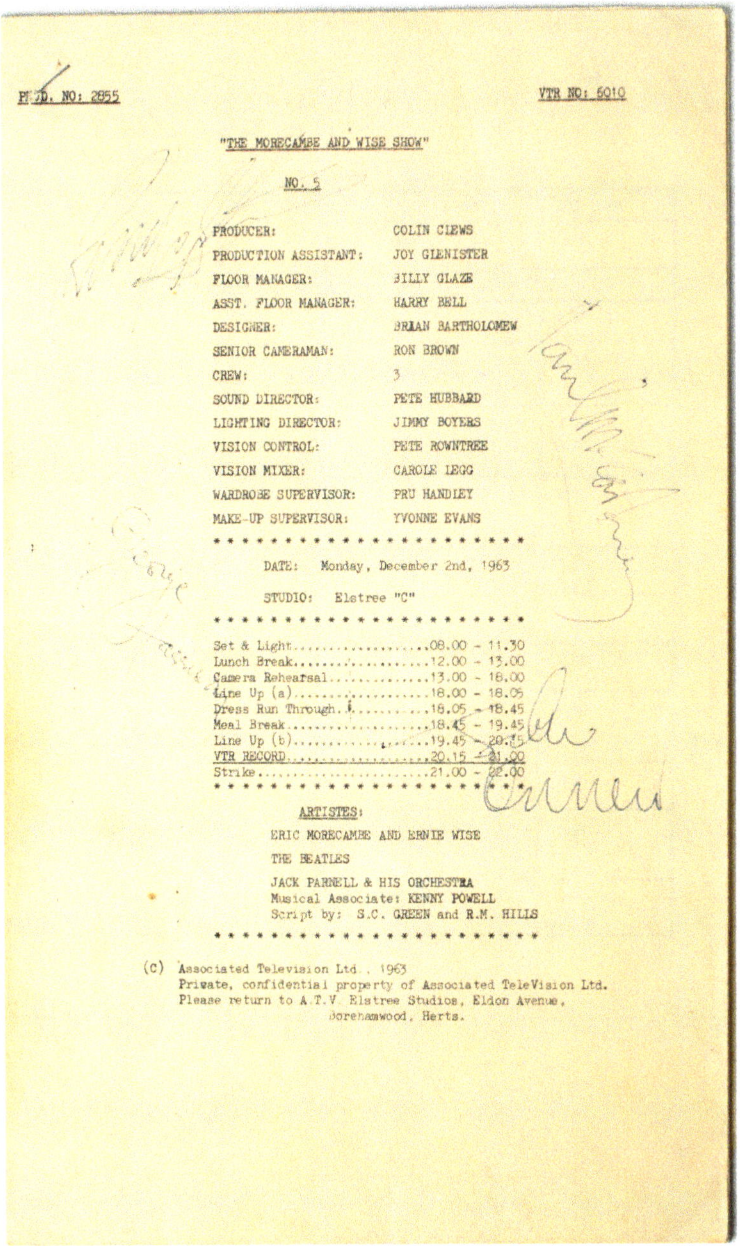

The Beatles Looking Back: The Final Trip

A script for The Morecomb and Wise Show *from December 1963, which has been autographed on the front page by all four Beatles. In addition to their performance of their hits, they also performed, in jest, "On Moonlight Bay" with the hosts of the show.*

The Beatles Looking Back: The Final Trip

Top left, The Beatles Fan Club card signed on front by all four.

Top right: A clipping from a UK newspaper magazine promoting The Beatles coming to America signed by all four Beatles.

Bottom right: Extended play (EP) UK 7" record cover titled "All My Loving" signed on the reverse by all four Beatles in 1964

The Beatles Looking Back: The Final Trip

The following pages feature a notebook that was turned into a Beatles scrapbook. It includes pictures with handwritten lyrics of The Beatles' songs.
What makes this book a true one of a kind is each page that includes a picture has been individually signed very nicely by John Lennon, Paul McCartney, "Best Wishes from" George Harrison, and Ringo Starr with an additional McCartney signature on the back cover (he also wrote Beatles underneath).

If that isn't enough, the group looked through the book and Paul made a correction on the lyrics for "P.S. I Love You" in his own handwriting (he crossed out a line and added "these few words till we're together". Another correction was written in for "Twist and Shout" He added "up" three times instead of "a" and also crossed out what the scrapbook's creator had written. This is an incredible and historical item I proudly owned in my collection.

The Beatles Looking Back: The Final Trip

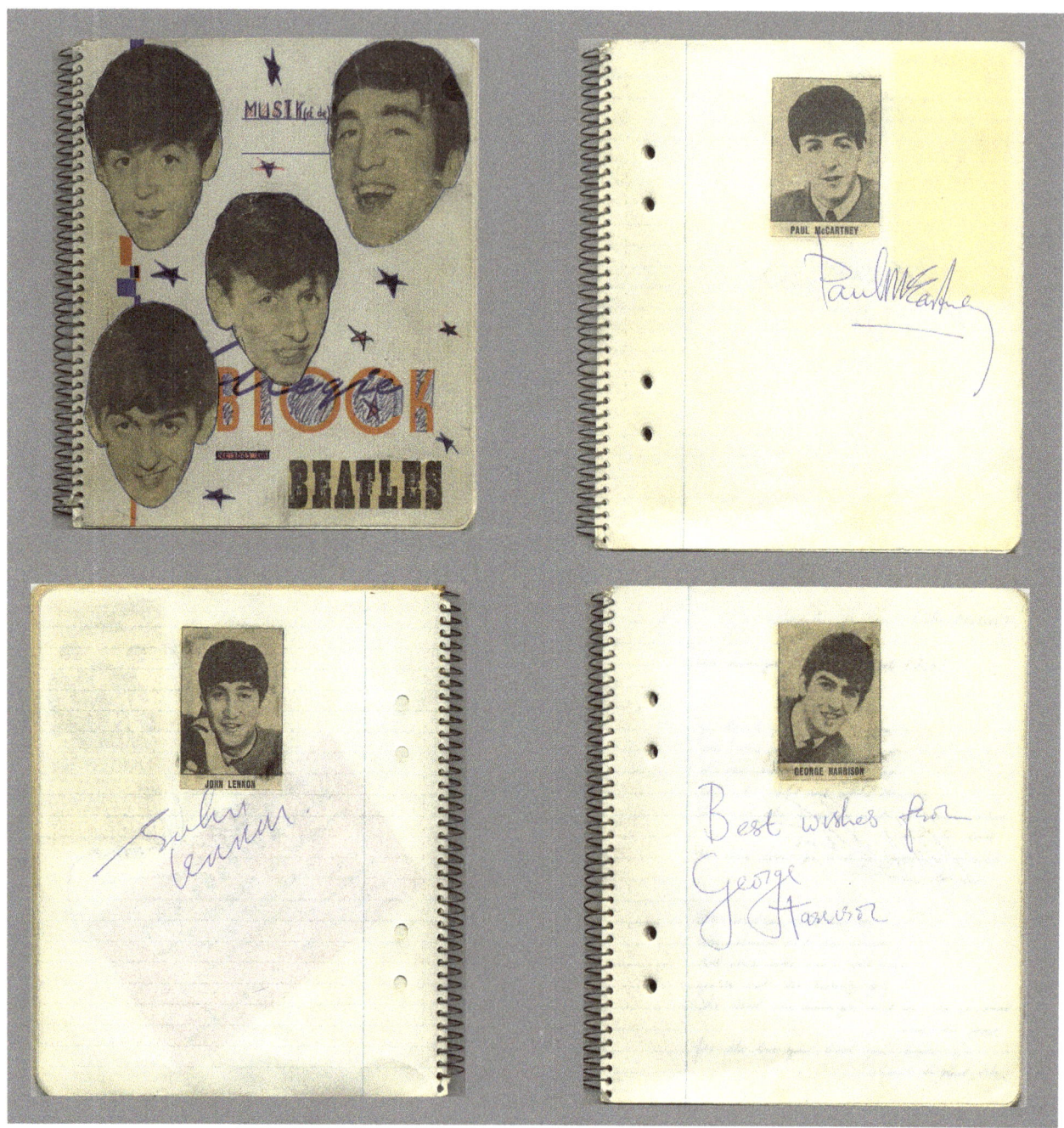

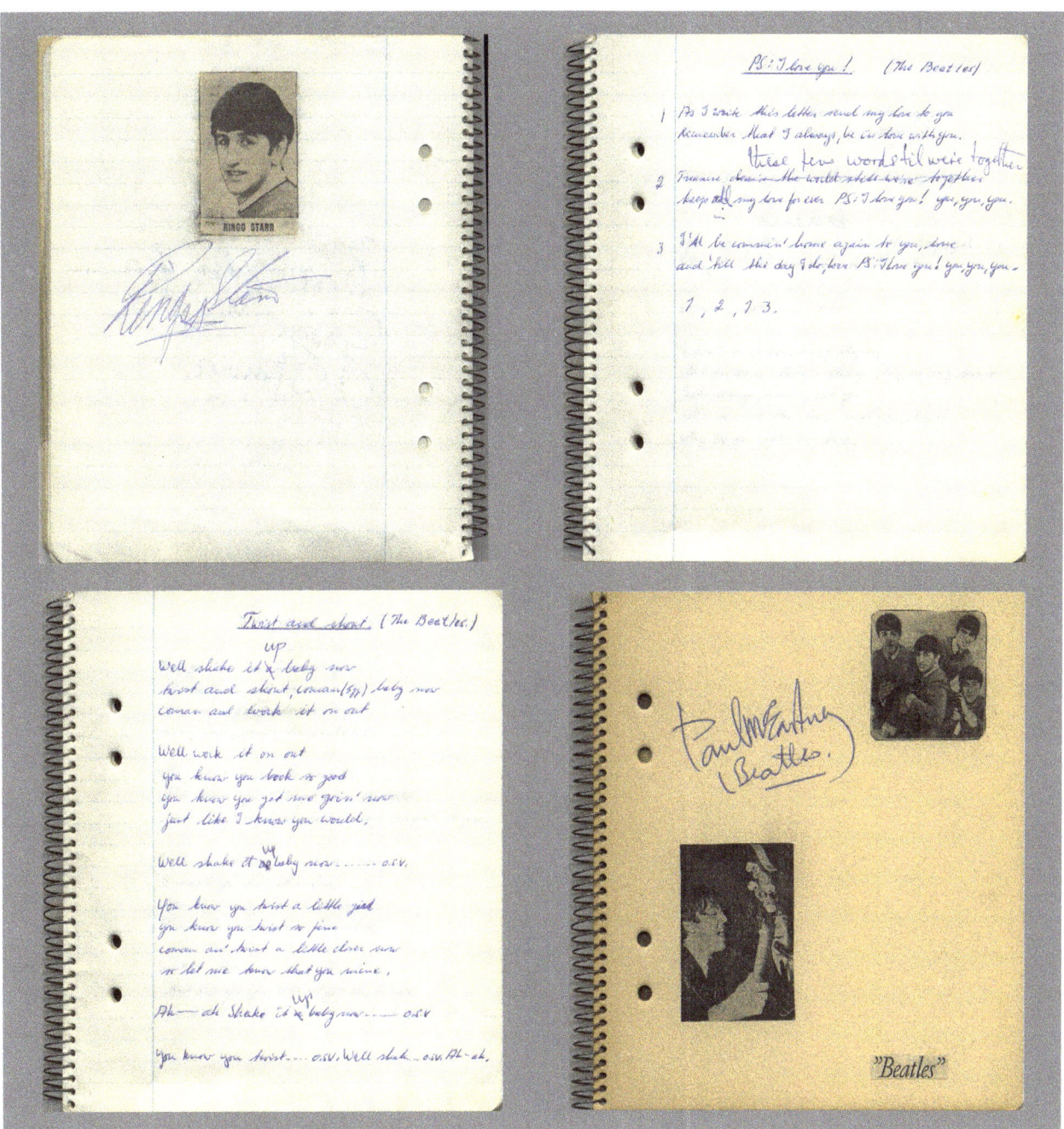

The Beatles Looking Back: The Final Trip

with the beatles *UK album cover signed on the reverse by all four.*

THE BEATLES FIRST FLIGHT TO AMERICA FEBRUARY 7, 1964

A Pan American pilot's letter written on February 7, 1964, describing the flight and The Beatles. He obtained all four Beatles' autographs on a Pan Am postcard before they landed in America for the first time. This was one of my prized possessions

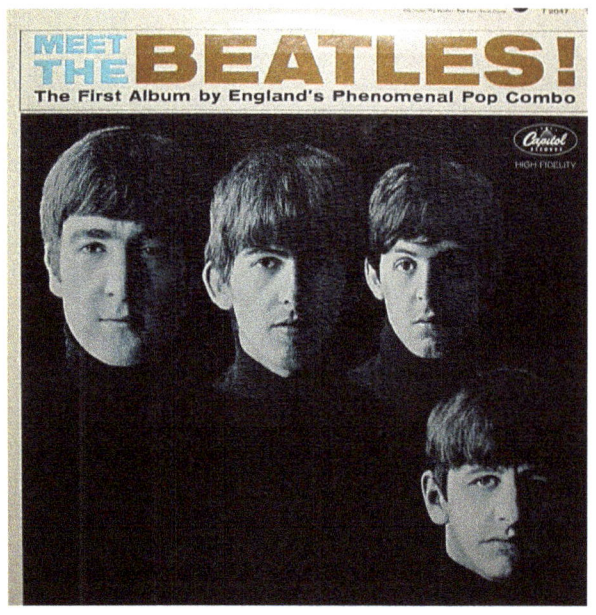 

Meet the Beatles *Capitol Records album cover signed on the reverse side. It was obtained in New York when* The Beatles *made their first US appearance on* The Ed Sullivan Show *on February 9, 1964 and authenticated by Lilian Eisen in the letter below.*

August 23, 2006

To Whom It May Concern,

The record album, Meet the Beatles, was signed for my brother Edward Stein. He worked as a lighting technician at CBS studios in New York City in the late 1950's to 60's. He worked on many shows and events, including What's my Line? and The Ed Sullivan Show.

Sincerely,

Lillian Eisen

Lillian Eisen

Meet the Beatles, *their first US Capitol album cover, signed on the reverse side by all four Beatles. This was also obtained on their first US visit.*

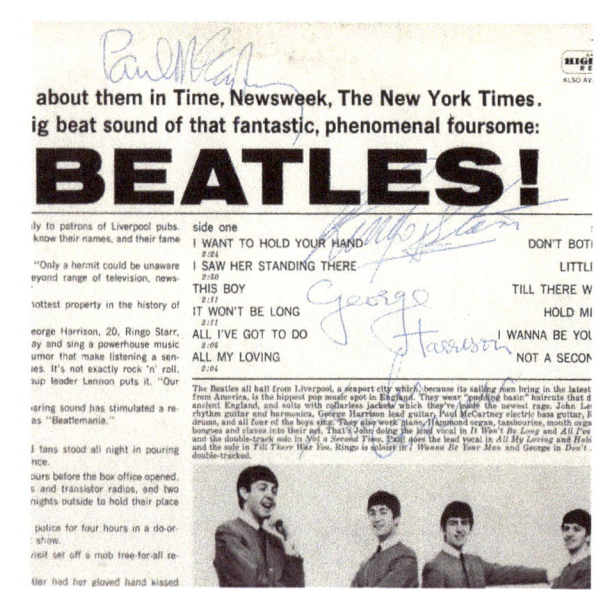

The Beatles Looking Back: The Final Trip

Dear Mr. Fontaine:

This is a history of my mother's Beatles autographs as I know it.

In 1964, my mother lived in Ft. Lauderdale, Florida. She had a girlfriend whose parents were in the music industry and they owned a yacht named the S.S. Ariadne. While in town for the Miami show the Beatles borrowed the yacht. The autographs came from the group while they were there with the yacht.

I hope the information above helps you.

Sincerely,

Regina Jarvis

A set of autographs by all four Beatles signed while they were in Miami, Florida, in 1964, during their first U.S. visit. The signatures were obtained by the recipient during a yacht trip with The Beatles as they took a break from rehearsing and preparing for their live appearance on the Ed Sullivan Show *on Sunday, February 16 1964.*

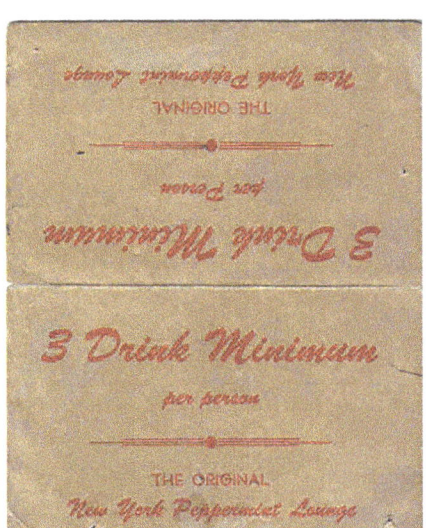

A drink card from the New York Peppermint Lounge in Miami. Inside the card is signed by all four Beatles, February 1964. Manager Brian Epstein gave these signatures to a waitress who served them drinks, and I obtained them from her.

The Beatles Looking Back: The Final Trip

A 1964 Peppermint Lounge Postcard from New York signed by Paul McCartney and fellow band mate Ringo Starr during their first trip to America in February of 1964.

On the other side of the Atlantic, also in 1964, Paul McCartney and Ringo Starr have signed on the reverse of a post card from the Royal Landcaster Hotel in London. Paul has also drawn a early example of his face, something he would do often after The Beatles disbanded in 1970.

A rare 8x10 of the well-known promotional photo by Dezo Hoffman showing The Beatles in their famous collarless suits, signed by all four.

The Beatles Looking Back: The Final Trip

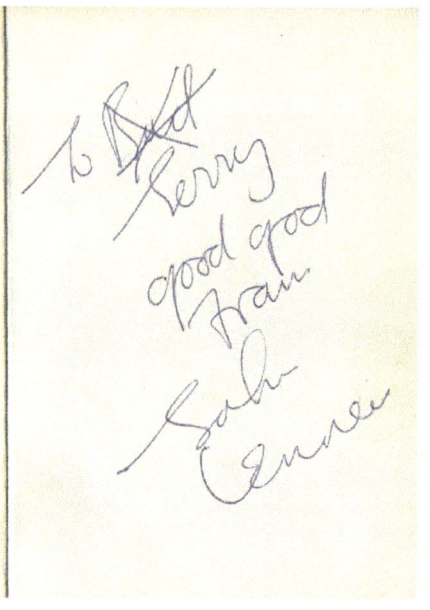

John Lennon's book, In His Own Write, *signed on the inside by all four Beatles, with annotations by all.*

Below, signed by all four on inside cover page from 1964.

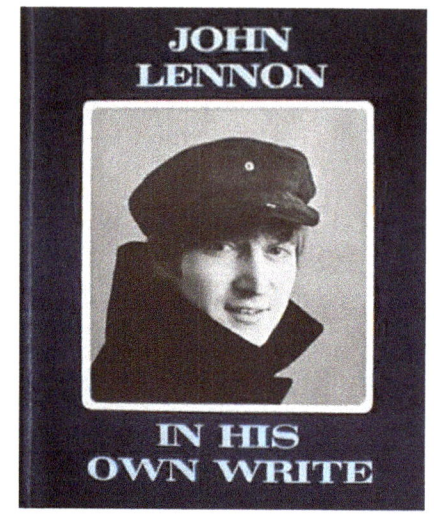

Another rare 1964 8x10 promotional Dezo Hoffman photograph showing The Beatles in another pose wearing their famous collarless suits, signed by all four.

A menu from The Variety Club of Great Britain's Show Business Awards luncheon, signed by all four Beatles on March 19, 1964.

When John accepted their award he said, "Thanks for the purple hearts."

Ringo quickly corrected him, saying, "They're silver."

In response, John quipped, "Sorry Harold (speaking to Prime Minister Harold Wilson).

Lennon was in good form on this day

Original 8-1/2x11 flyer for a closed circuit television presentation of The Beatles first concert, which took place in Washington, DC, on February 11, 1964. This pre-recorded presentation was offered in Long Beach, California, on March 14 and 15. Also on the broadcast were The Beach Boys and Lesley Gore, whose performances had been filmed at separate locations.

Proof Advertisement poster that was used for print ads promoting The Beatles latest single, "Can't Buy Me Love," on Capitol Records in 1964.

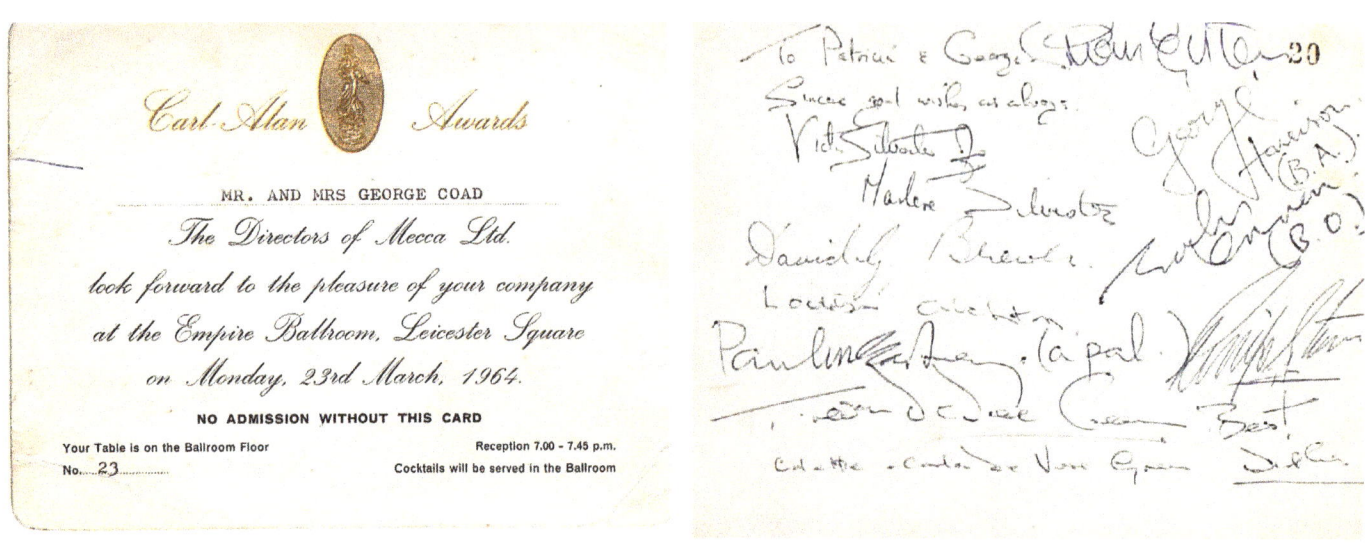

A Carl Allen Awards invitation ticket signed by all four Beatles and their manager Brian Epstein, along with other notable people who attended the event. Notice the number on the reverse is different from the front.

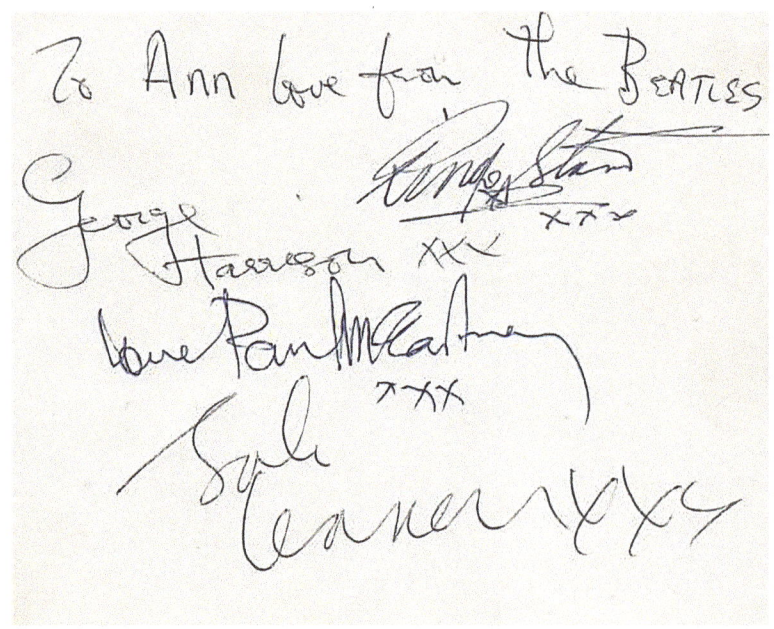

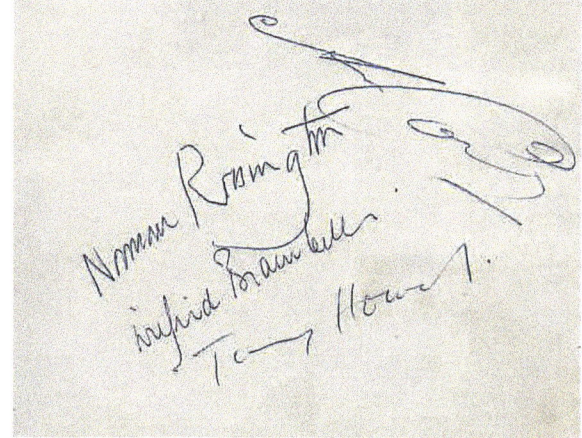

An ensemble of signatures from 1964 obtained during the filming of A Hard Day's Night signed and inscribed nicely by all four Beatles and co-stars from the film.

The Beatles Looking Back: The Final Trip

In-flight menu signed by all four Beatles on the reverse in 1964. Menu shows image of France and was printed in the USA.

The Beatles Looking Back: The Final Trip

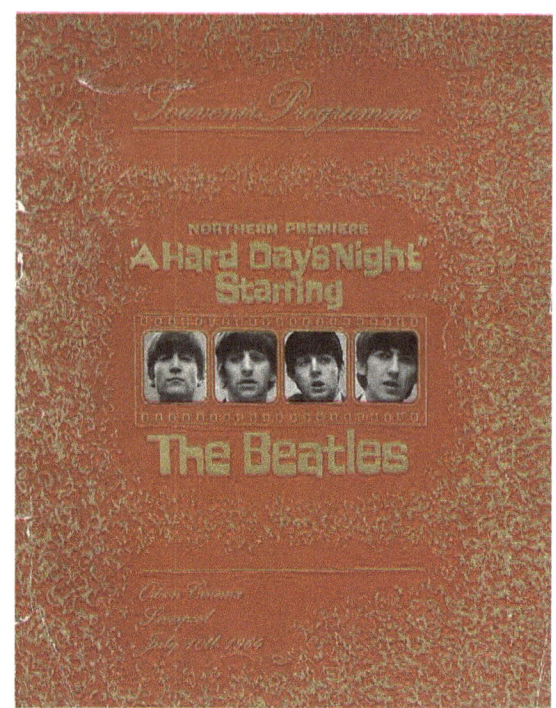

A souvenir program for the Liverpool Premiere of A Hard Day's Night, *signed on the inside page by all four Beatles, as well as Juke Box Jury host and personality David Jacobs who was on the flight with The Beatles.*

This poster is one of only two produced announcing the closure of the Blenheim Lounge on July 10, 1964 due to a press conference involving the The Beatles, who were in Liverpool to promote their film A Hard Day's Night. The Beatles straight from the airport to the Lounge, where they answered reporters' questions about the movie, etc. All four Beatles added their signatures to this sign!

This piece was originally mounted on a hardwood backer but was later removed from that and placed on acid-free linen backing for preservation. It is truly remarkable that this sign survived for almost sixty years! In addition, several pictures were taken of The Beatles arriving at the airport and another that was taken in the lounge. There was also a video made documenting this day in Liverpool.

The Beatles A Hard Days Night *U.K album cover featuring the songs from the film, signed with dedication by Paul McCartney at the top and all four's signatures at the bottom. John's signature, although a little smudged, includes an arrow pointing to his picture below. These signatures are from 1964.*

The recipient's handwritten note about her experience was in pencil and difficult to read, so it has been transcribed:
Beatles — got to station at 4:25, had coffee had fab publicity with Skitch-Mirror Express, got on train at 20-9. Beatles got on at Westbourne Park at 8:45. Producer, Walter Shenson, me, George, John, not so nice ,George out of this world. Paul came and spoke to me for 3/4 hour, lunch 1/2 passed 12.

> This is to certify that the accompanied autographs of the Beatles was obtained by me in 1964 when I had a small non speaking part in the film A Hard Days Night. I was 16 at the time and was one of the schoolgirls in the train sequence.
>
> *[signature]*
>
> Ann Armstrong

A nice set of signatures obtained during a break from the train scene while filming A Hard Days Night *in 1964. See transcribed letter and typed letter signed by the recipient above*

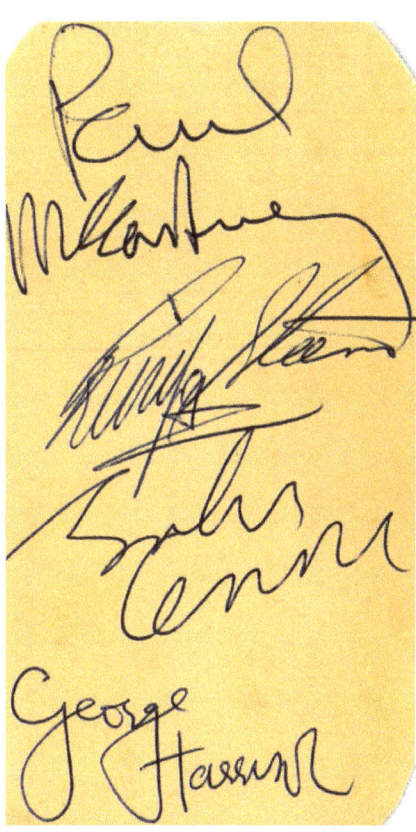

Oversized 12x16 sepia-toned photo of The Beatles off the negative signed by all four. What makes this extra special is that through correspondence with the recipient's family member, this photo was tacked on the wall on the set of A Hard Day's Night, then removed and signed by all four. Very rare.

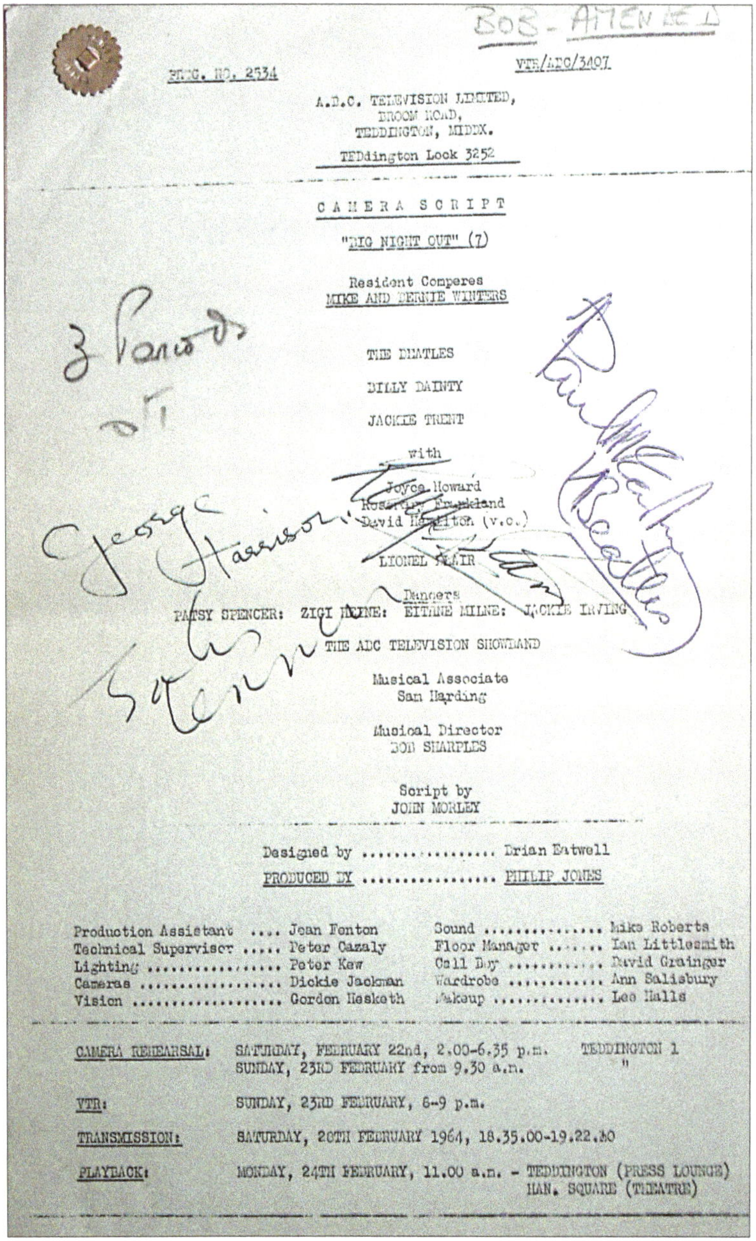

The Beatles Looking Back: The Final Trip

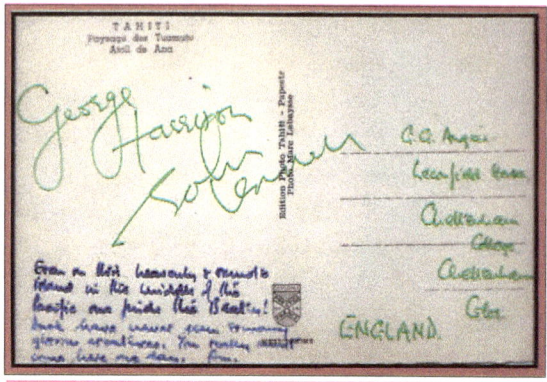

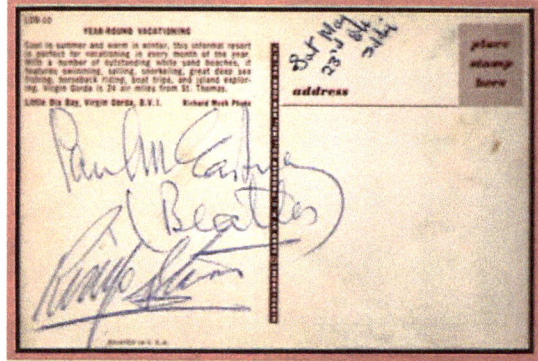

An original script for the show Big Night Out *(summer of 1964), featuring The Beatles. It is signed on the front by all four.*

A unique set of autographs obtained while all four Beatles were on holiday at the same time, in different locations.

John and his wife, Cynthia, along with George George and his girlfriend, Patti Boyd, went to Tahiti. A lucky fan was able to get a postcard nicely signed by John and George, and penned her memories of the meeting (top).

Paul McCartney and his girfriend at the time, Jane Asher, and Ringo Starr with his girlfriend, Maureen Cox, went to the Virgin Islands. Another lucky fan obtained their autographs and dated them at the top (bottom).

To my knowledge, this is the only set of signatures signed by the four while they were on holiday.

A South Pacific Teal Flight Companion magazine signed by all four Beatles and their tour press agent Derek Taylor during a flight from their New Zealand tour in 1964.

Capitalizing on The Beatles craze, a London radio station held a contest in 1964 where the prize was spending the day with The Beatles. The winner, A.F. Prescott, asked the Beatles to sign the consent form.

 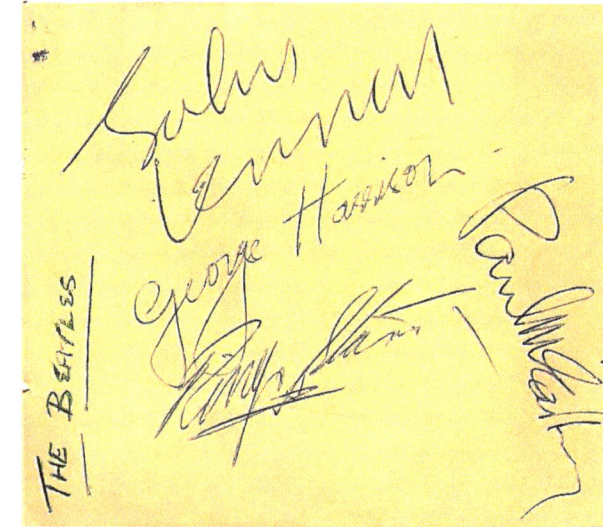

Two nice autographs taken from autograph books from 1964.

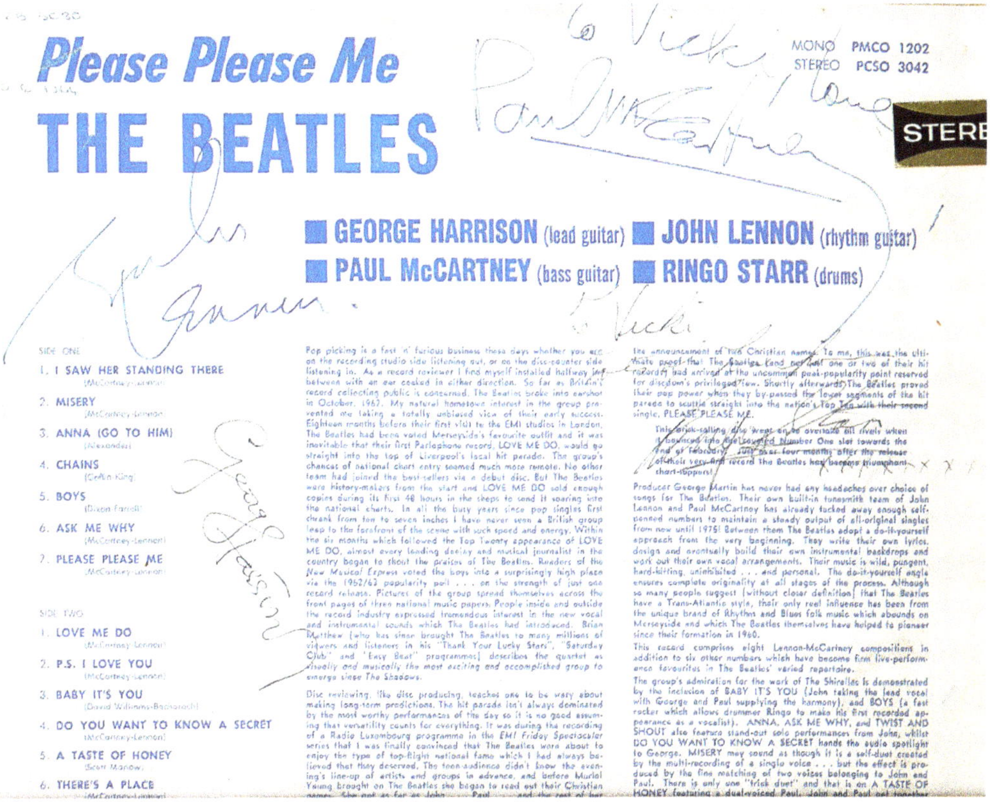

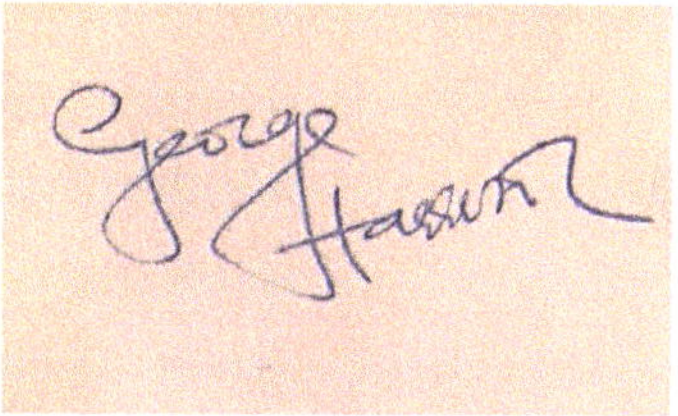

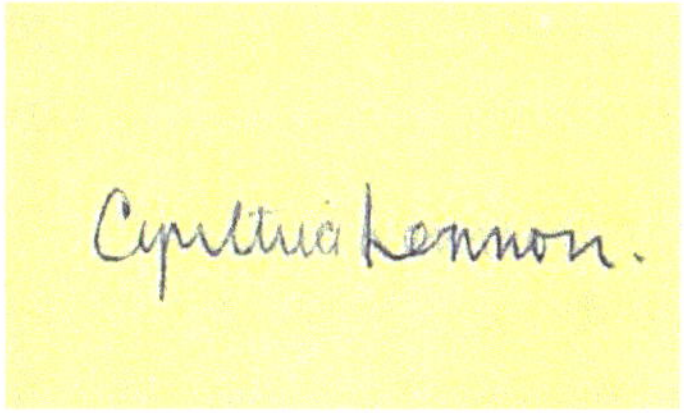

The Beatles Looking Back: The Final Trip

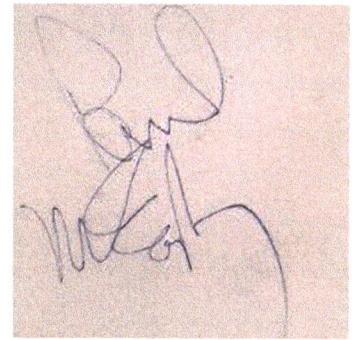

Top left, an extremely rare Australian pressing of *The Beatles album* Please Please Me signed on the reverse side by all four Beatles. Obtained in 1964 during their Down Under Tour in New Zealand and Australia.

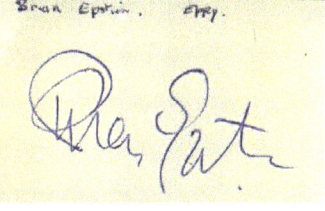

The signatures shown here are all from an amazingly star-studded autograph book, which includes signatures from John Lennon, Paul McCartney (twice), George Harrison, Ringo Starr, Brian Epstein (The Beatles' manager), Roadie Mal Evans, Cynthia Lennon, Patti Boyd (George's then girlfriend, signed twice), Jane Asher (Paul's girlfriend, signed twice), Jimmie Nichol, replacement drummer for Ringo while he had his tonsils removed (rare), and British singing duo, Peter and Gordon. Featured here is a sampling of the signatures from this book.

The Beatles Looking Back: The Final Trip

A mini 1964 Beatles calendar that is signed on the inside by all four. Very cool!

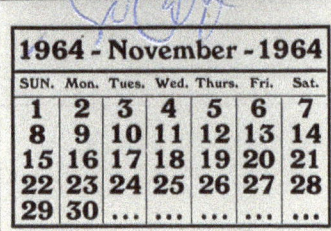

A nice set of signatures from a 1964 autograph book.

A candid polaroid photo showing all four Beatles, which signed nicely on the reverse side by all four members of the band.

The Beatles Looking Back: The Final Trip

A nice set of signatures provided by all four Beatles while the visited the home of the recipient. A commemorates the visit. This was uncommon because The Beatles had such a tight schedule that they rarely got to do anything else. (I purchased these directly from the owner.)

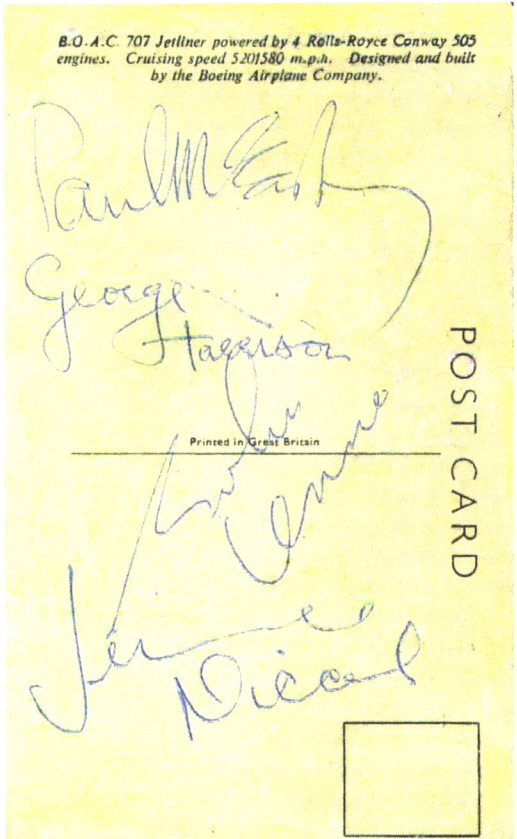

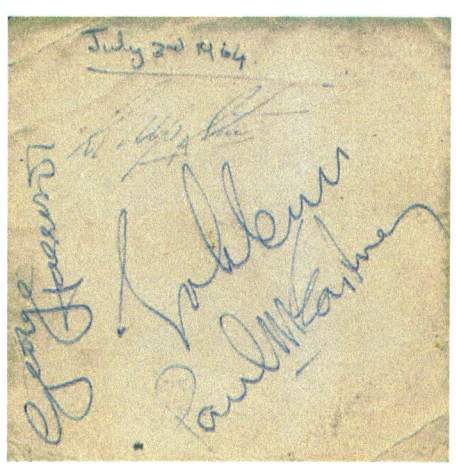

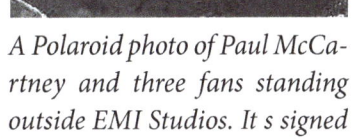

A Polaroid photo of Paul McCartney and three fans standing outside EMI Studios. It s signed on the reverse side by all four Beatles on July 2, 1964. It's rare to see in this form.

Left, A rare set of The Beatles autographs adorns this postcard. It was signed by Paul, George, John and drummer Jimmie Nicol, who replaced Ringo on some of the dates during The Beatles' Down Under tour in 1964 because Ringo had to have his tonsils removed. (Ringo was back with the band by the time they performed in Melbourne.)

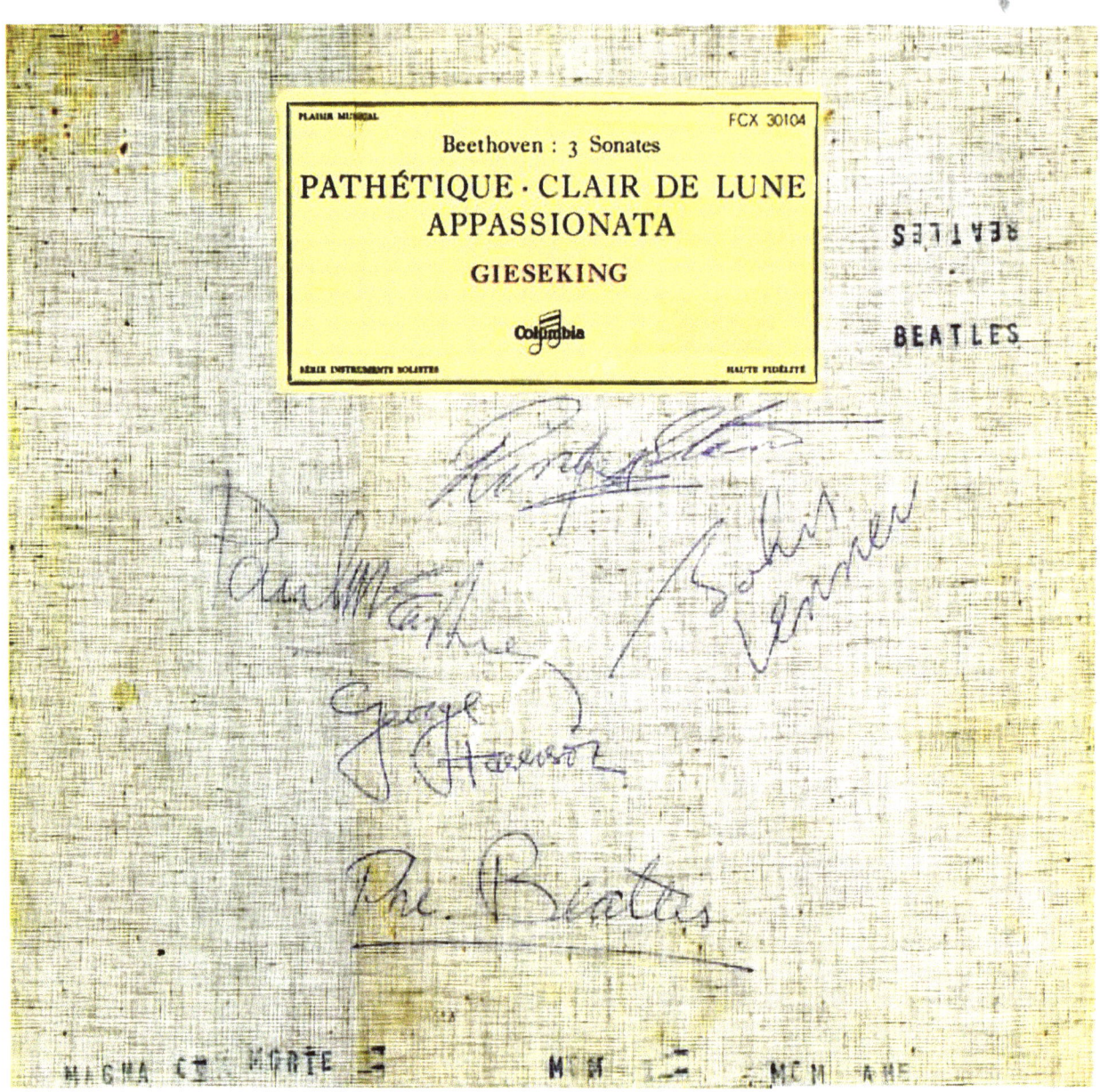

When you have an opportunity to meet the Beatles and ask for their autographs, sometimes the only thing you have for them to sign a Beethoven album. They did record "Roll Over Beethoven," so maybe that was the recipient's inspiration for having them sign this particular item. It's certainly unique!

The Beatles Looking Back: The Final Trip

Left, Beatles manger Brian Epstein's handwritten itinerary, listing locations and dates for The Beatles' 1964 US tour written on both sides of an envelope.

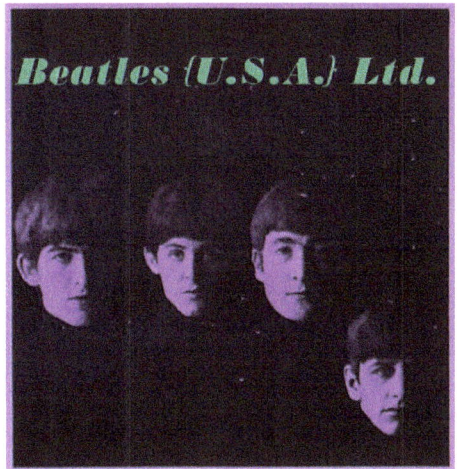

Right, concert program signed on the inside first page by all four Beatles. This was obtained on their first U.S. summer tour in 1964.

RIAA sales award Gold record presented to The Beatles in 1964 for the song, "I Feel Fine".

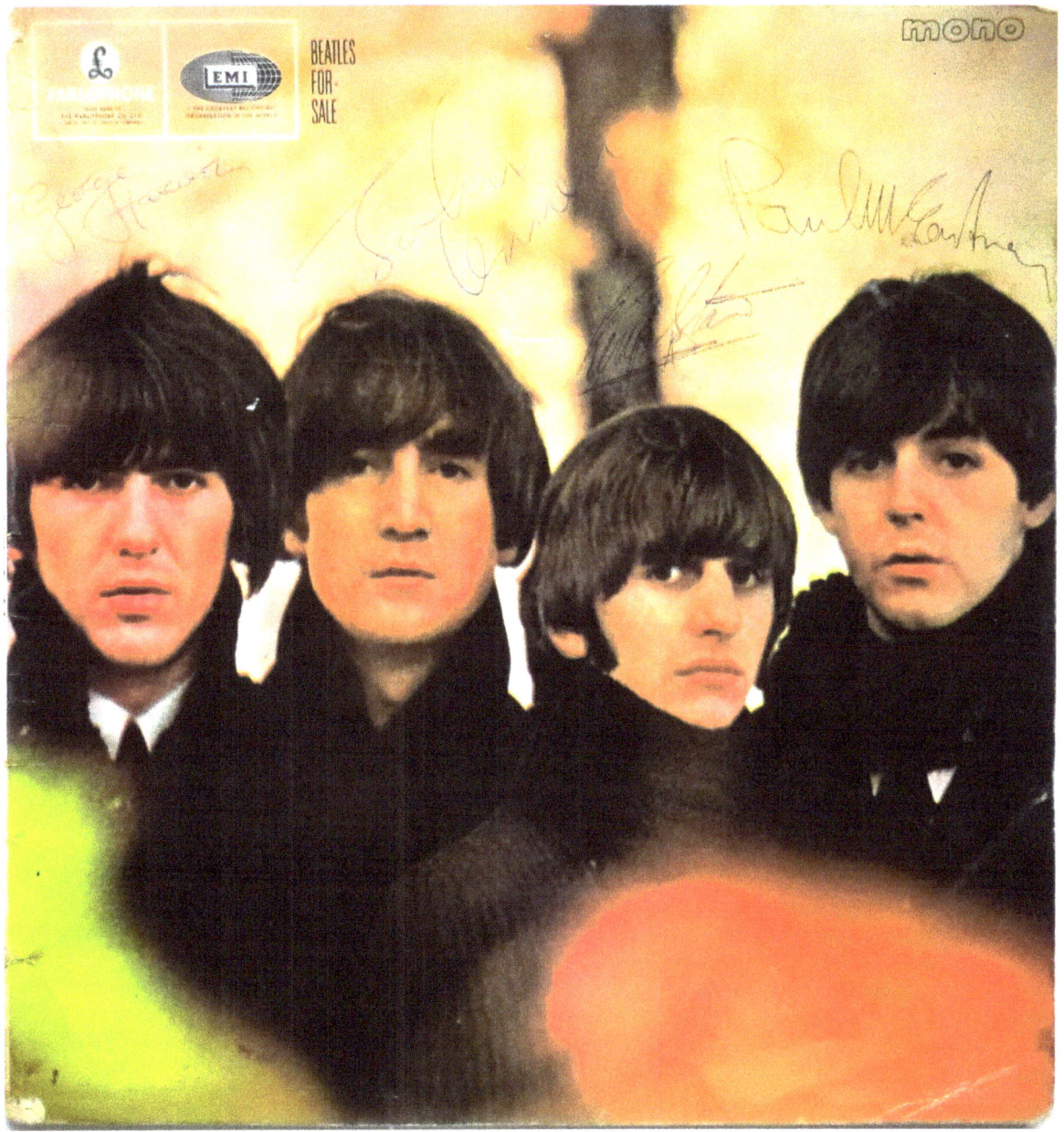

Extremely rare Beatles For Sale *album cover signed on the front by all four Beatles in late 1964. Less than half a dozen of these particular album covers are known to be signed in this manner.*

The Beatles Looking Back: The Final Trip

A Best Wishes card from The Beatles to fan club Secretary Ann Collingham, signed by all four. 'm not sure why George wrote to Mary, possibly that was her real name. It is a little tongue and cheek however, as Paul wrote Collingham for his last name. It was all good fun.

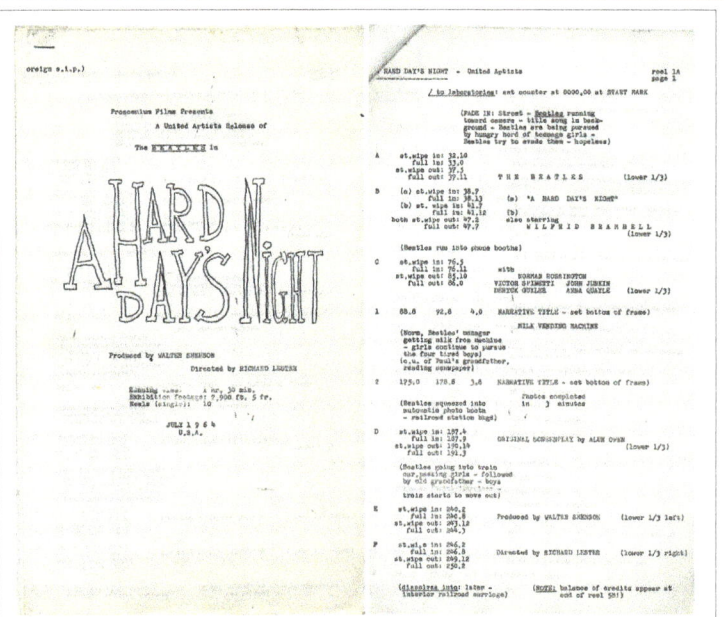

Original Projection Script for The Beatles motion picture A Hard Day's Night from 1964.

Original script for the Beatles second movie, Help! Since there was no title at the time, they gave it the working title Beatles Two.

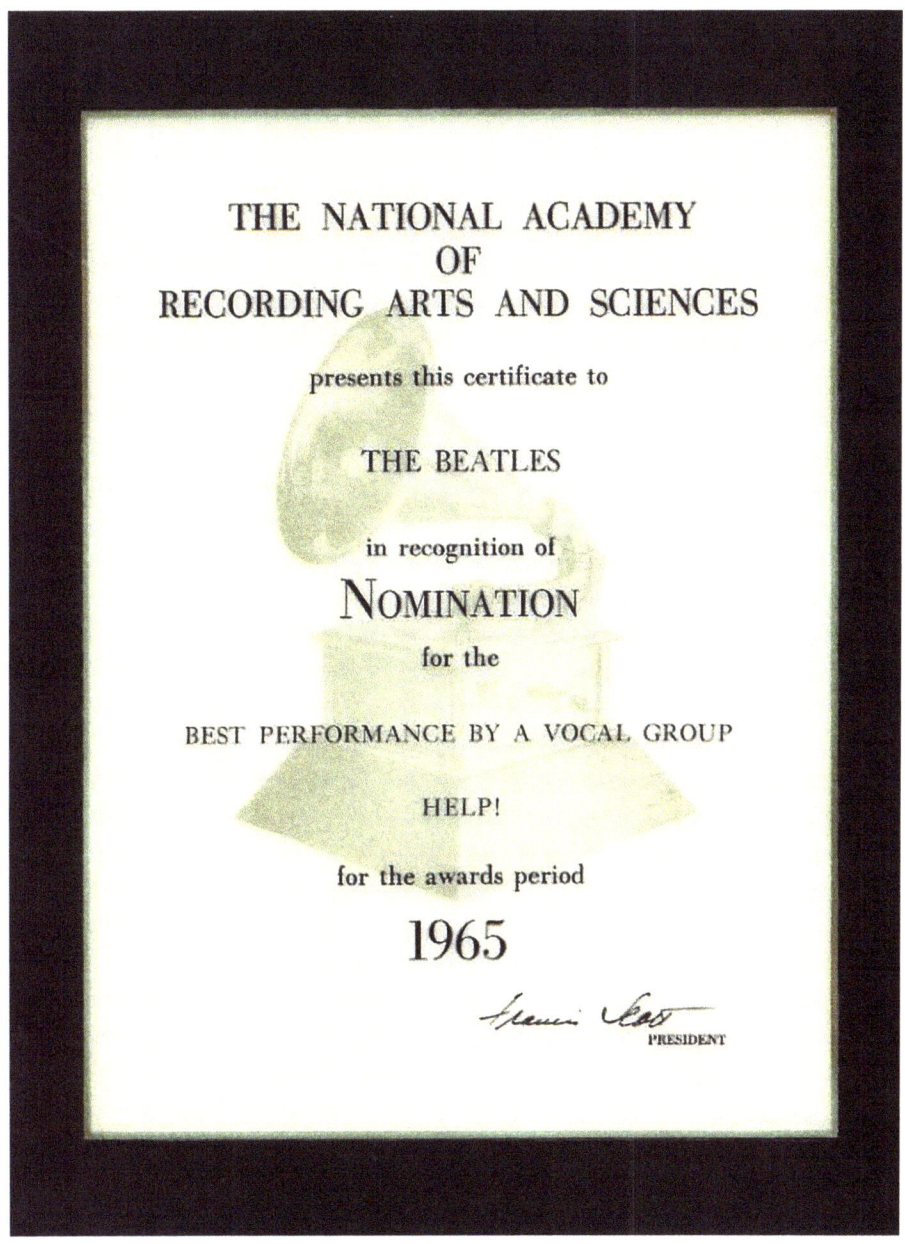

Grammy Nomination Plaque certificate given to the Beatles in 1965 in recognition of the best performance by a vocal group. It was earned for the title song from their second movie, Help!

An 8x10 photo of the Beatles in the Bahamas from 1965 when they were filming their movie, Help! It is signed by all four, plus the director of the film, Richard Lester.

The Beatles Looking Back: The Final Trip

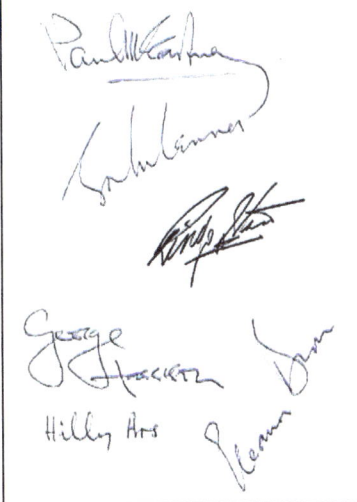

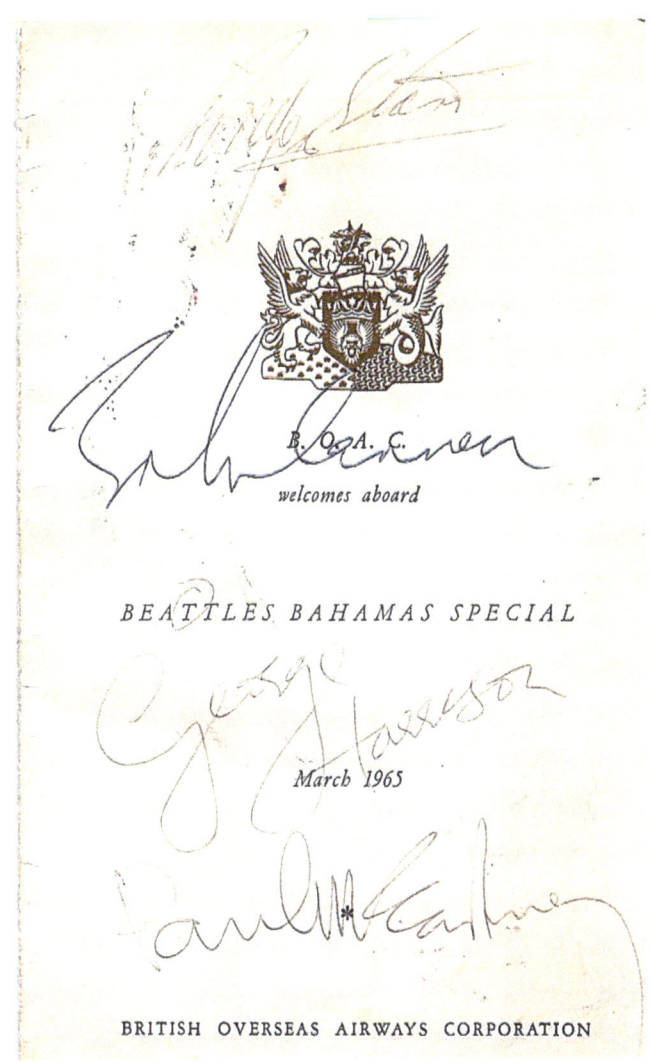

On February 22, 1965, The Beatles boarded a specially chartered Boeing 707 BOAC-Cunard for a flight to The Bahamas, via New York, to start filming their second feature film Help! A special in-flight menu was created for the trip, which was titled "Beatles Bahamas Special." The menu is signed on the back cover by all four Beatles and their Help! co-star Eleanor Bron. Paul McCartney has also humorously signed as 'Hilly Ars", a fictional character he made up.

Beatles Bahamas Special menu signed during the flight back from to the Bahamas in March 1965 when filming their movie Help! This particular menu has a spelling error on the word Beattles, which one of the band members noticed and circled.

Victor Spinetti's fur hat worn, far left, during the Austrian winter scenes, as shown here, in the movie Help!

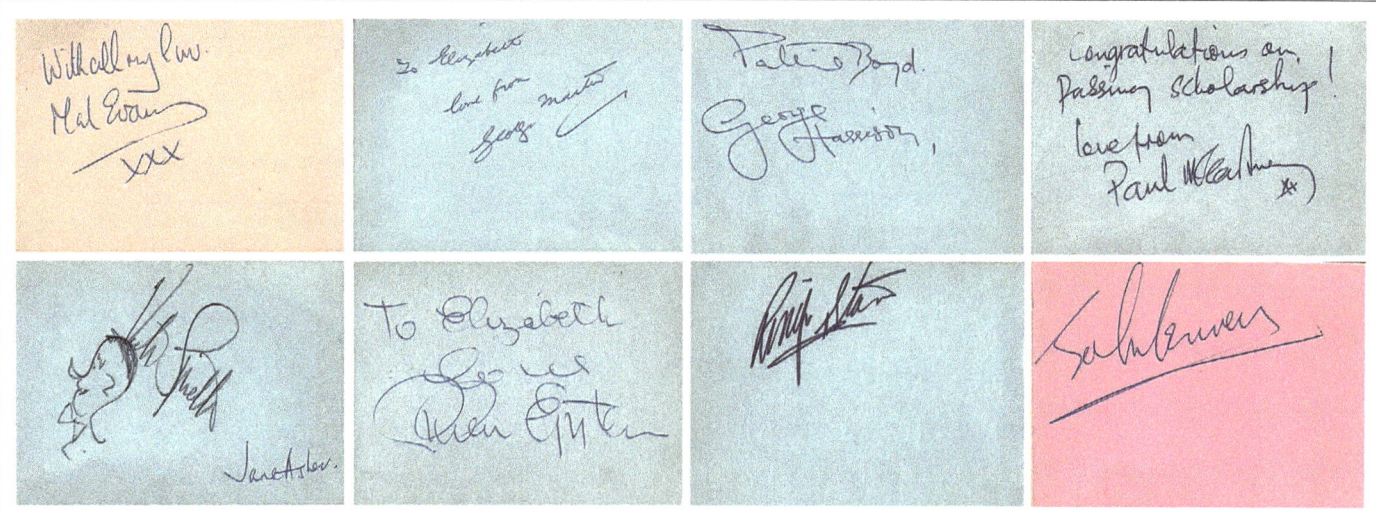

The above signatures came from an autograph book. The signatures of all four Beatles, road manager Mal Evans, producer George Martin, manager Brian Epstein, Paul's girlfriend Jane Asher and Help! *co-star Victor Spinetti were included. The book was signed in 1965 during the time* Help! *was being filmed.*

The Beatles Looking Back: The Final Trip

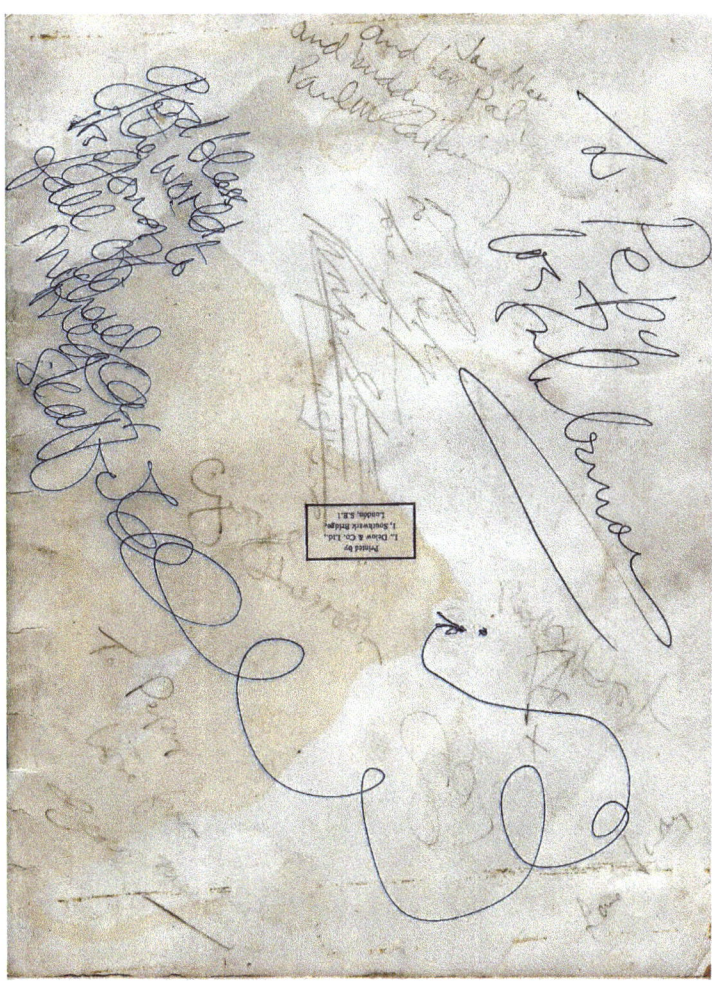

This is a Royal World Premiere program for the movie Help!, which premiered on Thursday July 29, 1965. On the reverse the program is dedicated to Pat Preston, fondly known to band members as Pepy. It is signed by John Lennon in black ballpoint pen, Jane Asher, and Paul McCartney, who signed it as her "pal and buddy". George Harrison signed: To Pepy, and Ringo Starr wrote: To Pepy, love from George Martin and love Judy (Martin). Members of the Scaffold all signed in pencil, and due to age some of these pencil signatures are difficult to see. Paul's brother, Mike McGear, also from The Scaffold, has dominated the program by signing in blue ballpoint pen.

The Beatles Looking Back: The Final Trip

A nice set of signatures obtained at the 1965 Poll Winners Concert at Wembley Arena in England. The original ticket to the even and a press photo accompany the signatures..

The Beatles Looking Back: The Final Trip

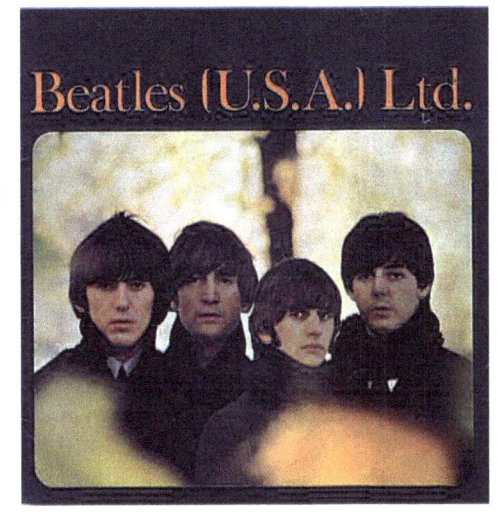

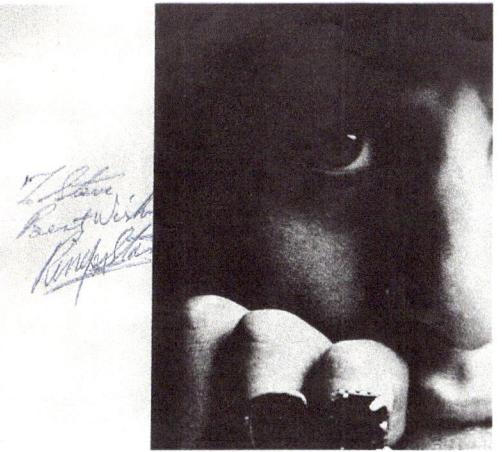

A 1965 Beatles US Tour program, signed inside with inscriptions by all four Beatles. This was signed to Steve, a discotech dancer in one of the opening acts for the tour.

Tony Barrow's official crew press ID card for the August 1965 US tour. Barrow was press officer for The Beatles.

The Beatles signed this photo on a hot August night in Los Angeles when they met their idol, Elvis Presley. This photo was signed to Billy Smith, who was Elvis's cousin, who is also featured on the following page.

The Historic One-Time Event — The Beatles Meet Elvis

IN 1965 THE BEATLES CAME TO CALIFORNIA. WHILE THEY WERE THERE THEY VISITED ELVIS AT HIS HOME AT 525 PERUGIA WAY BEL AIR. I, MY WIFE JO, AND OUR SON DANNY LIVED WITH ELVIS AT HIS HOME. WE WERE FORTUNATE TO MEET AND TALK WITH EACH OF THEM. ALSO WE WERE ABLE TO OBTAIN THREE AUTOGRAPHS FROM EACH ONE OF THEM. I OBTAINED TWO AUTOGRAPHED PICTURES.

BILLY SMITH

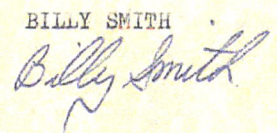

The Beatles Looking Back: The Final Trip

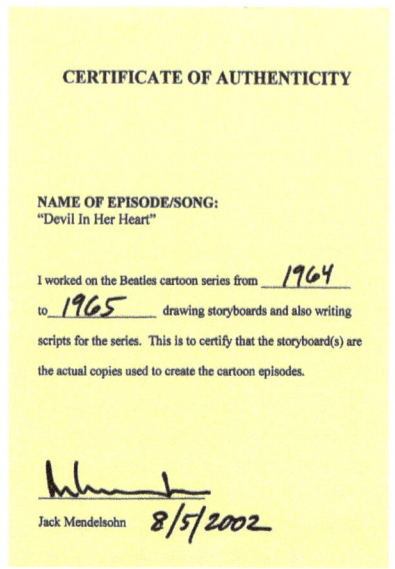

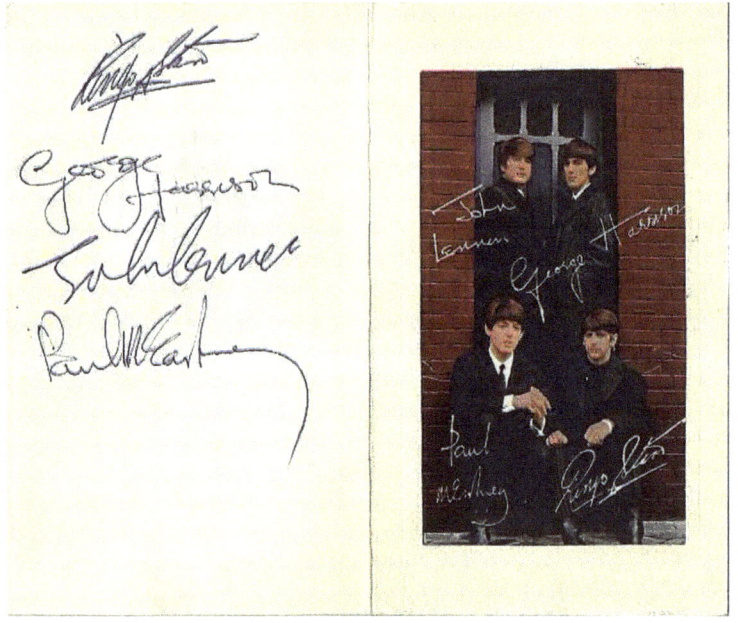

Top left and right, *series drawing storyboards from The Beatles Cartoon and a written script.* These are the actual drawings used to create the episodeds. I was able to obtain more than a dozen storyboards, and each was accompanied by a signed letter from Jack Mendelsohn. Notice the title on the storyboard is not the title given to the cartoon when it was aired. They renamed each episode to reflect that song that was used. This particular episode was renamed "Devil in Her Heart". These are really rare.

Bottom left, *a nice set of signatures from 1965 inside a photo folder showing an early image of The Beatles.*

The Beatles Looking Back: The Final Trip

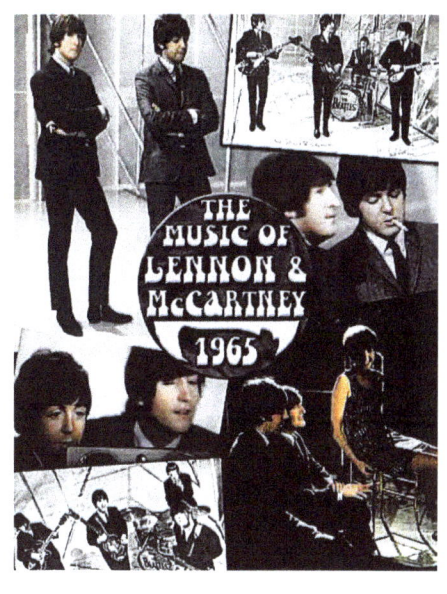

The Music of Lennon & McCartney show's call sheet for a 1965 TV special is signed by John and Paul, as well as other artists who appeared on the special. These included Marianne Dunbar (Faithfull) and Cilla Black. These autographs were signed on November 2, 1965.

The Beatles Looking Back: The Final Trip

A color magazine photo picturing The Beatles at the Speedway Golf Course in Speedway, Indiana in September 1964. It was signed nicely by all four circa 1965-66.

The Beatles Looking Back: The Final Trip

A Kuwait Airways sticker with the peel off signed by all four Beatles on the plane during their trip to Manila in 1966.

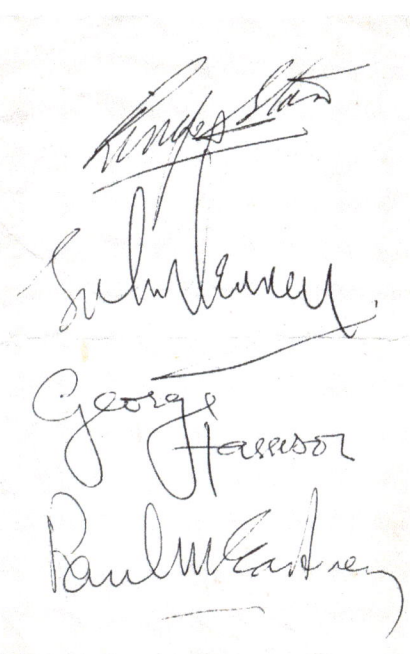

"The Beatles autographs were obtained for me by my aunt in 1966. She lived in Los Angeles and was employed by a public relations company who worked within the Music Industry. They promoted artists and events. And organized particularly EMI."

— Steve Criswell
August 2013

Pan Am postcard signed on the reverse by all four Beatles in 1966.

American Airlines postcard signed on the reverse by all four Beatles and manager Brian Epstein in 1966.

The Beatles Looking Back: The Final Trip

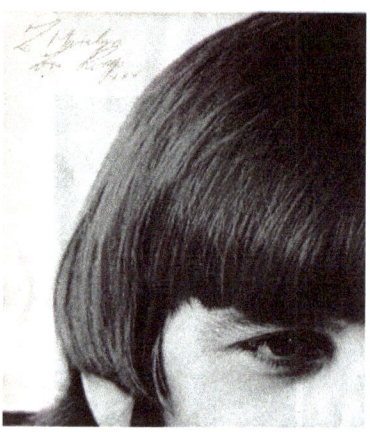

Marilyn Doerfler, helped promote Beatles

ALANA BARANICK
Plain Dealer Reporter

Marilyn Doerfler, who died Thursday at age 69, professed to have paid teenage girls $1.50 apiece to scream wildly when the Beatles landed at LaGuardia Airport in New York City in February 1964.

As a member of the promotion team for the Fab Four's American tours in the mid-1960s, Doerfler placed ads in smaller newspapers outside the city. She sought swooners to cause a commotion for her English invaders as their counterparts had done for Elvis Presley and Frank Sinatra in the decade before.

The then-married mother of three traveled with John Lennon, George Harrison, Ringo Starr and Paul McCartney across the states from 1964 to 1966. Each day, she interviewed them on tape, then fed her recorded conversations to radio stations by phone. She also penned promotional articles about the rock band for teen magazines.

In 1980, she told The Plain Dealer's Jane Scott that she felt closest to John "because he had the best sense of humor. He was always way ahead of the others." She kept in touch with him until his death.

"I liked George a lot too," she told Scott. "He was a softie. He looked serious, but every now and then he'd flash a smile that would warm your heart. Ringo was fun. Paul, though, was the hard nut. The best-looking. The glamour boy. The best showman on stage."

Doerfler also worked for Apple records for two years. She helped with the Monterey Pop Festival and toured Europe with the vocal group the Association.

After moving to the Cleveland area in the early 1970s, she did public relations work for some local bands and songwriters. She later handled bookkeeping for some commercial property management companies.

The Cleveland resident died of complications after colon surgery at MetroHealth Medical Center.

Doerfler, whose maiden name was Williams, was born in Detroit. She spent her teen years in Pittsburgh.

While working as a secretary for Pittsburgh Paints, she served on a committee that assigned imaginative names to various shades of paint colors.

Impressed with her creativity, her boss took her to New York during the winter of 1963-64 to meet Brian Epstein, who managed the Beatles and was looking for a woman to join the promotion crew for the upcoming tour. When Doerfler asked Epstein what his product was, he said, "Beatles."

"I gave him a disgusted look," she told Scott. "I thought he meant bugs."

Doerfler, who at one time showed purebred cats in competition, volunteered with the Humane Society. Memorial donations may be made to the Humane Society of the United States, 2100 L St. N.W., Washington D.C. 20037.

She is survived by her daughters, Karen Bhagwat of Farmington Hills, Mich., and Lisa Dorow of North Ridgeville; a son, Stephen of Gilbert, Ariz.; and 11 grandchildren.

Services will be at 10 a.m. today at Liston Funeral Home, 36403 Center Ridge Road, North Ridgeville.

To reach this Plain Dealer reporter:
abaranick@plaind.com, 216-999-4828

This Beatles 1966 US Tour Program is signed inside and inscribed to Marilyn Doerfler. Each Beatle signed next to his respective image. Marilyn, who was a journalist and interviewed the group for various magaines, traveled with the Beatles on all three of their US tours. Included here is an obituary write up that appeared in The Plain Dealer *after her death on Feb. 17, 2005.*

Due to age, the inscriptions are not easy to read, so I'm including the text for each here:

To Marilyn, without whom, l ots of love and everything ….from him John Lennon (he also drew a crucifix, which was tongue in cheek and related to the controversy surrounding his "We're more popular than Jesus" statement).

To Marilyn, from your cousin in law Paul McCartney

To Marilyn, love from George Harrison Thank you Girl (reference to the 1963 Beatles song and he also drew a flower)

To Marilyn, love Ringo xxx

The Beatles Looking Back: The Final Trip

On August 29, 1966, The Beatles played their final concert in San Francisco's Candlestick Park. On this day, they autographed an official National League baseball for Mike Murphy, an employee of the San Francisco Giants organization. He gave the ball to his sister Anna right after he received to make up for not being able to get her tickets to the concert.

What a gift it was! It wound up being one of the rarest Beatles artifacts in their history, especially since it was connected to their very last concert performance.

Mike, who started as a bat boy for the Giants in 1958, was their clubhouse assistant manager when The Beatles performed that cold, windy night at the park in 1966. He later became the clubhouse manager and held that position until Candlestick Park was torn down in September of 2015. After that, Mike became the Giants' senior advisor and in January of 2023 he announced his retirement after 65 years with the Giants organization.

I added this ball to my collection in 2005, and kept it until it was sold at auction many years later.

The Beatles Looking Back: The Final Trip

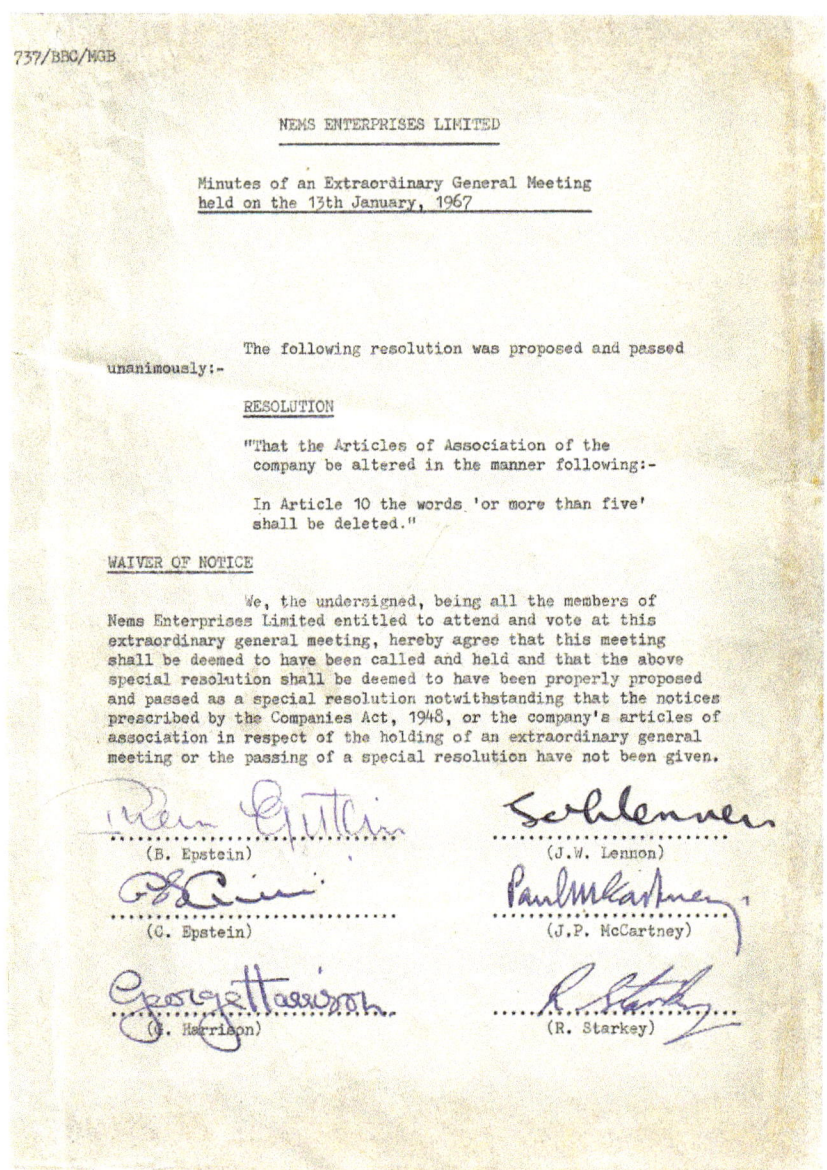

Very rare contract from Nems Enterprises signed by all four Beatles, manager Brian Epstein, and his brother, Clive Epstein, in January 1967. This is one of the last documents signed by The Beatles and Brian collectively. He was doing very little with the band by this time, since their final tour ended in 1966. Brian paassed away later that year, so this 1967 document is a true artifact from Beatle history.

Sgt. Pepper's Lonely Hearts Club Band album cover signed in the center fold by all four Beatles. The signatures were obtained in 1967 by Apple Scruff girl, the late Lizzie Bravo. I've included a picture of Lizzie with John the night he signed the album (lower right corner).

This is a nice ensemble of three Sgt. Pepper album covers with signatures on the front obtained from the 1970s through the 1990s. From left to right, #1 is signed by John Lennon and Ringo Starr, who dated his signature '97 and also wrote WOW; #2 is signed on the top by Paul McCartney; #3 is signed on the top by George Harrison. An ensemble like this is seldom seen.

The Sgt. Pepper *album's front cover is a collage of images of notable celebrities. Each image was glued onto a cut-out and these were used to create the final artwork. The Beatles were the ones who chose which individuals would appear on the cover, and actor Tony Curtis was one of those select few. I met Tony Curtis in 2007 when he was a special guest at the Some Like It Hot film festival in Illinois. I showed him the cut-out from my collection and he said he'd never seen it before. I asked him to sign it on the reverse side for me, and he did, adding this inscription: "The Beatles chose me for Sgt. Pepper, Tony Curtis". This is the only known original Sgt. Pepper cut-out that has been signed celebrity pictured. I had the pleasure of seeing Tony two more times after that, and the second time he was wearing a The Beatles Sgt. Pepper shirt! Sadly, Tony passed away on September 29, 2010.*

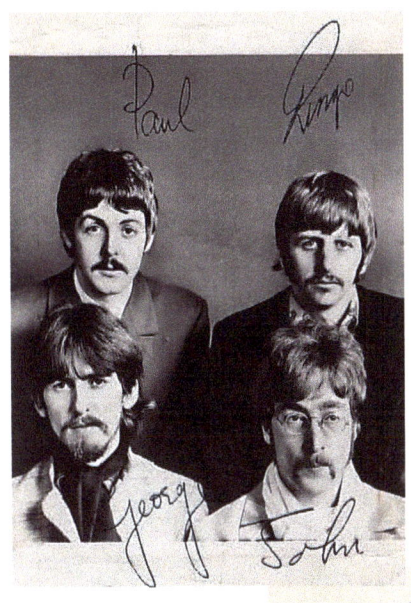

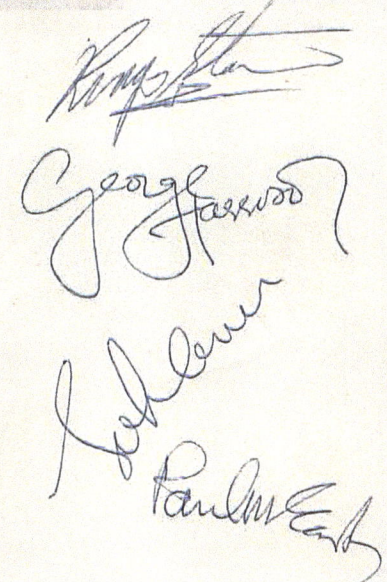

This Beatles promo photo card from 1967 has first name facsimile signatures on the front and is signed on the back by all four Beatles. This photo was obtained during the filming of Magical Mystery Tour.

These are two nice sets of signatures by all four Beatles that were obtained in 1967 during the filming of Magical Mystery Tour.

The Beatles Looking Back: The Final Trip

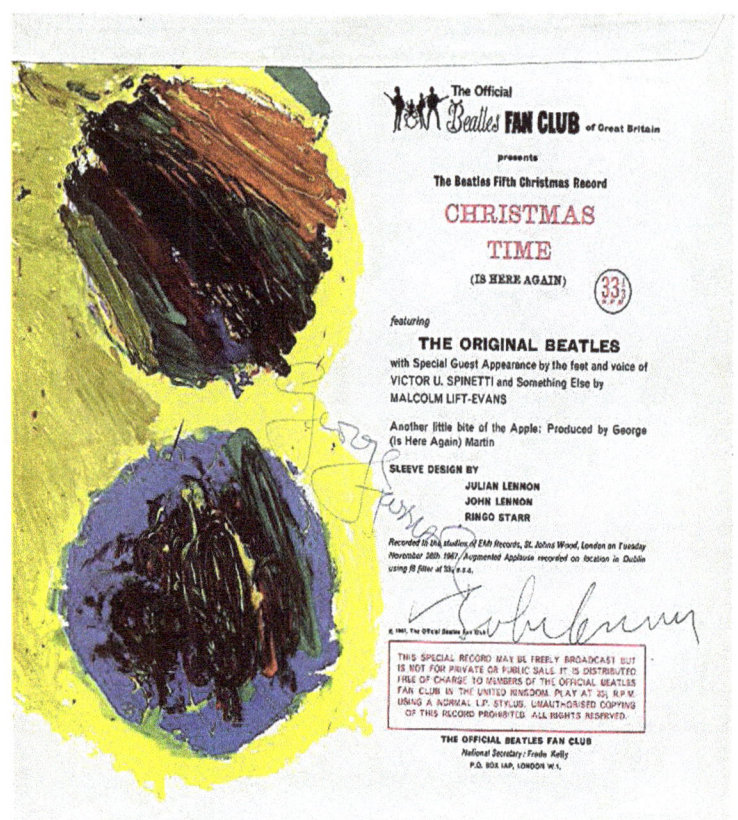

Beatles Christmas message to the fan club on flexi disc (record made of a thin, flexible vinyl sheet with a molded-in spiral stylus groove). The cover is signed on the back by John Lennon and George Harrison. These signatures were obtained during the private screening and reception for The Magical Mystery Tour. Below, John and George are pictured with some fans at the event.

An invitation from The Beatles to attend a private screening of their movie The Magical Mystery Tour in London on Dec. 17, 1967. It is signed on the back by John Lennon.

The Beatles Looking Back: The Final Trip

A set of posters from 1968, illustrated by artist/photographer Richard Avedon. They feature members of The Beatles individually. There was also a group poster that is not shown. These were only available for purchase through Look *magazine in 1968. As the years have gone by, these sets have become quite collectible.*

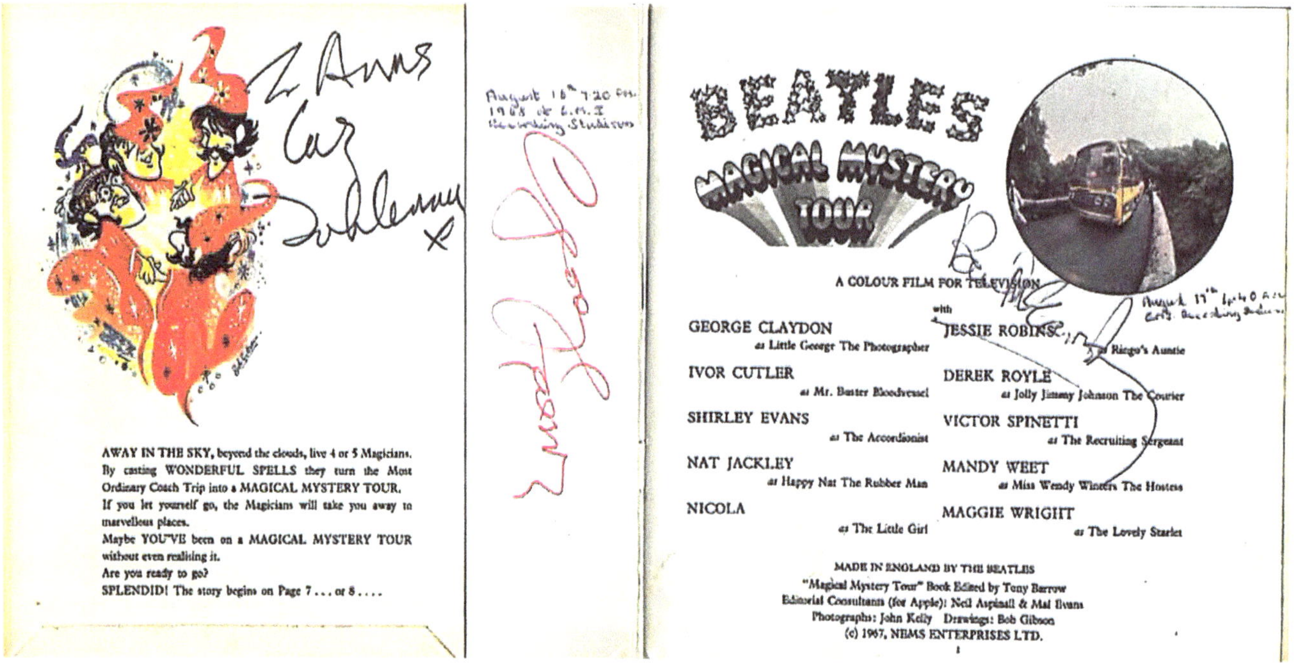

This *Magical Mystery Tour* British EP was signed by John Lennon, George Harrison, and Paul McCartney on different occasions in the 1960s. While in my possession, I sent Ringo Starr his photo from the booklet and told him that the EP was signed by all band memebers except him. A few months, later I received the signed page in the mail, which completed the set. (Ringo-signed image not pictured.)

Obtained in Bangor in 1968, this rare ensemble of autographs, again included signatures from John, George and Paul . They signed these when they were studying TM with the Maharishi Mahesh Yogi. These are accompanied by a nice card signed by Ringo that was obtained at a different time.

The Beatles Looking Back: The Final Trip

To Whom It May Concern

Re: Beatles Memorabilia

My Mother's employer was preparing to depart for India with the Brighton Transcendental Meditation Centre to the Maharashi Mahesh Yogi Centre. My Mother mentioned that I was still lamenting that I hadn't managed to obtain a whole set of signatures and her employer offered to take my autograph book with her just in case she was more successful. She managed to return with the 4 autographs together with two strands of John's hair as a gift for me.

I have kept these mementoes these past 35 years in a childhood memory box before deciding to sell them knowing that I will always have the memory and they will, no doubt, afford much pleasure to the recipient.

Yours faithfully

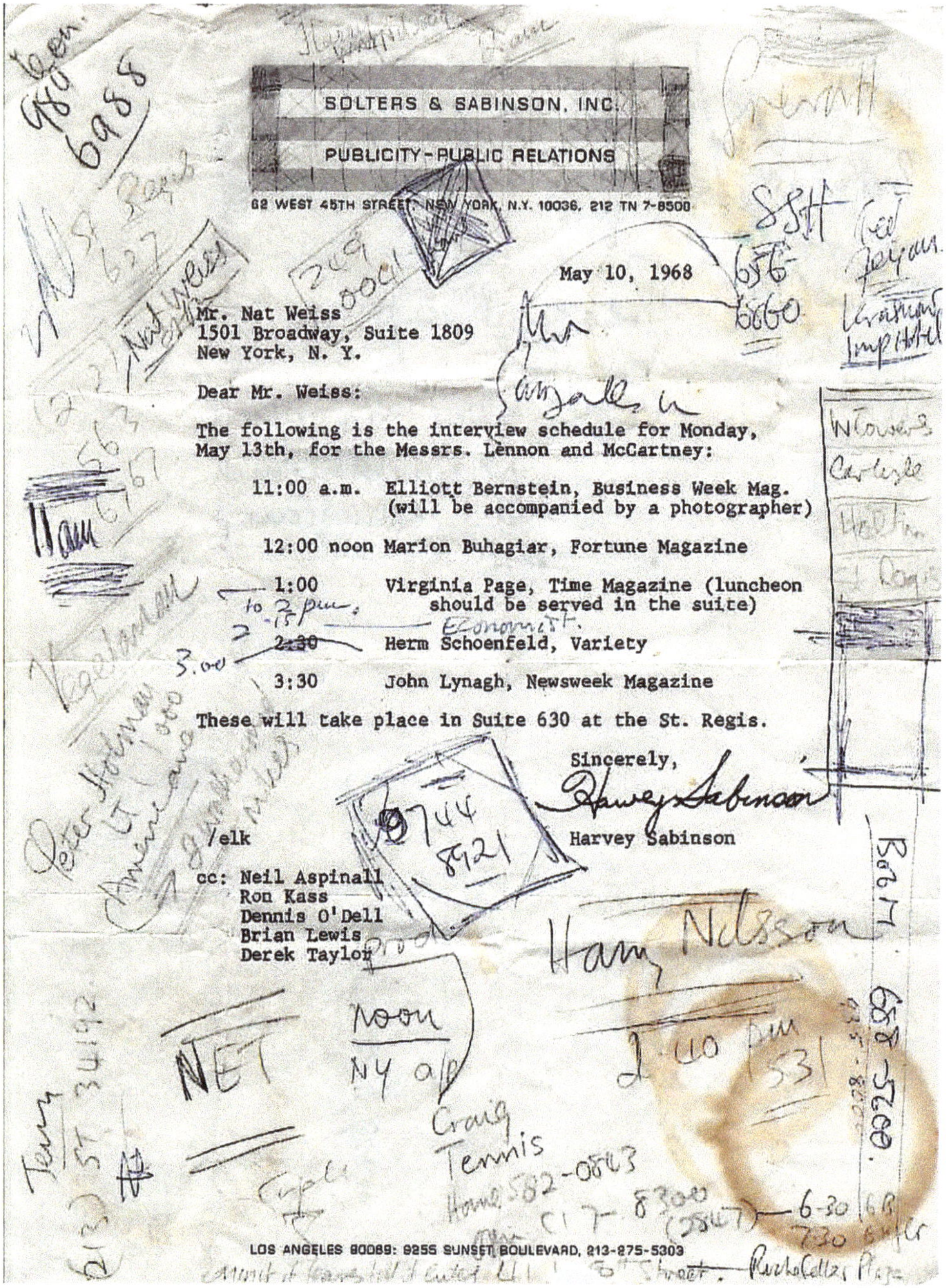

The Beatles Looking Back: The Final Trip

Looking at this, you might wonder why it's in The Beatles collection. If you look closer, this letter/itinerary dated May 10, 1968 includes writing, phone numbers, etc. It turns out it's a significant historical document both front and back because it came from the New York hotel room where John Lennon and Paul McCartney stayed when they announced Apple Records and also appeared on the Johnny Carson Show.

This piece includes many notations and phone numbers by both Lennon and McCartney, as well as others. Also on both pages are original negative proofs of Lennon and McCartney's arrival at the airport for this visit. What an incredible piece of Beatles' history documenting the thoughts and ideas they were having at that moment in time.

The front is seen at left, and the back is on the following page.

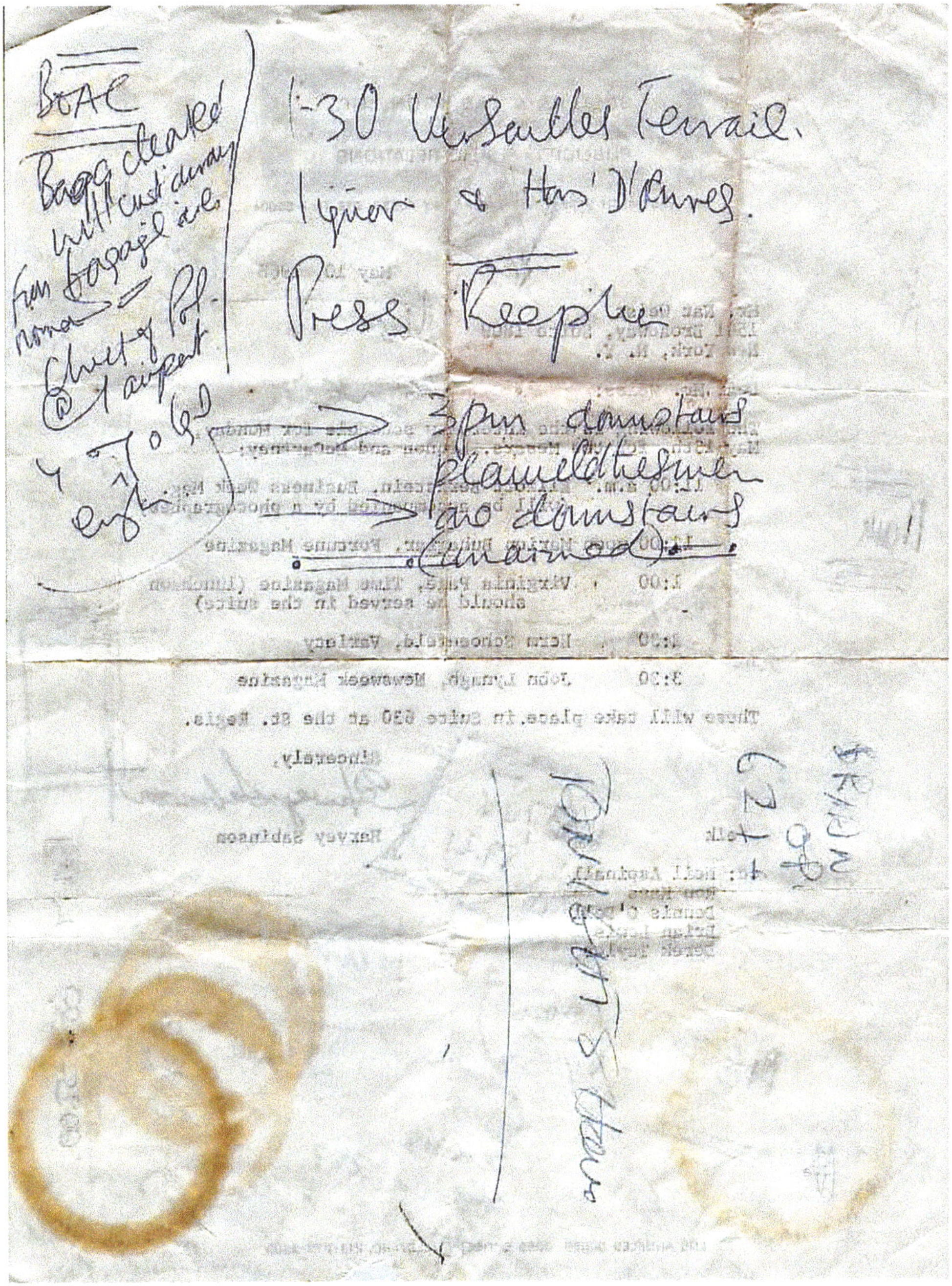

The Beatles Looking Back: The Final Trip

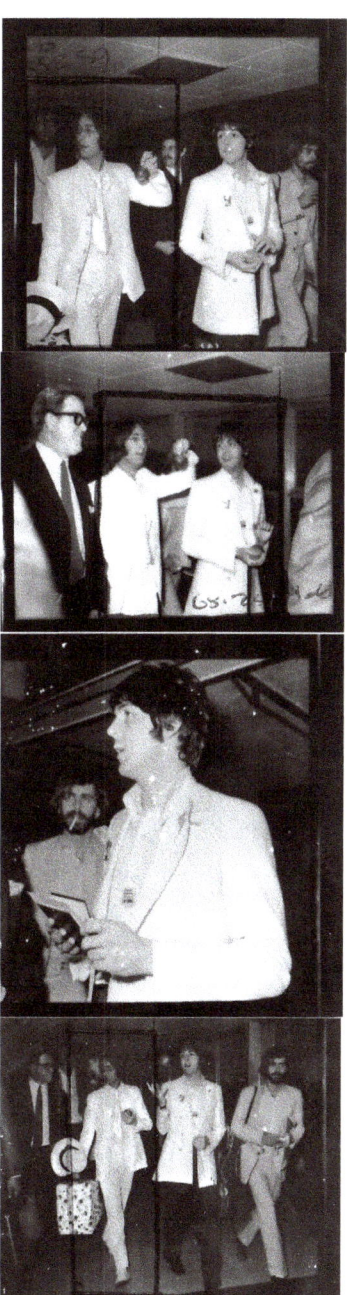

The Beatles Looking Back: The Final Trip

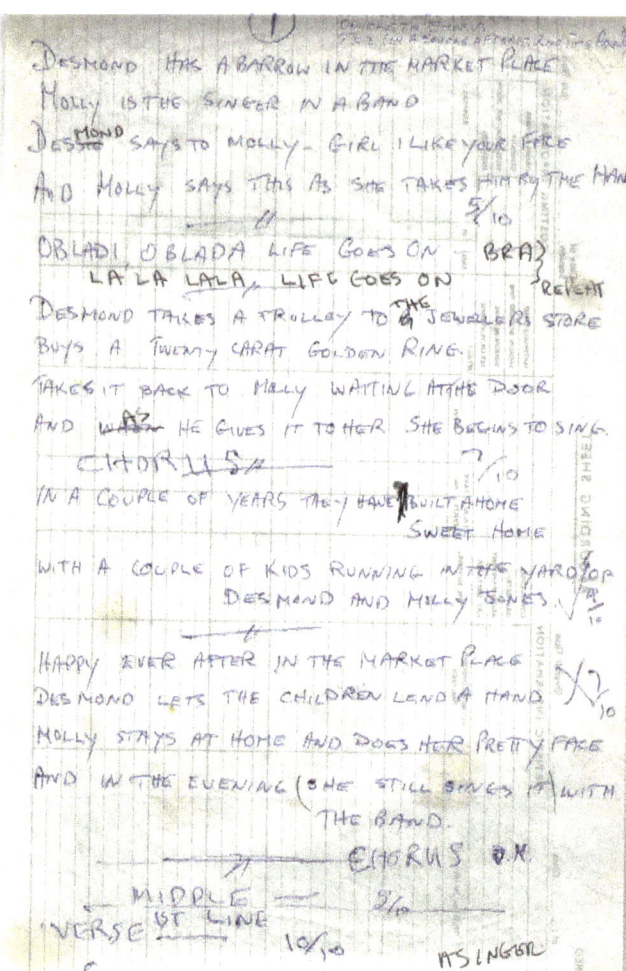

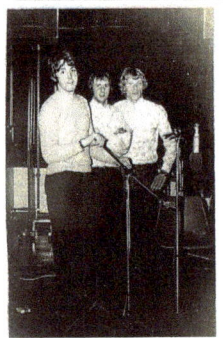

This handwritten letter by Beatle Paul McCartney, is from 1968 and is addressed to Keith Drewitt and Peter Dymond, also known as Drew and Dy, who were aspiring artists who wanted to record with Apple. Paul writes, "Our L.P. is going well now so something unexpected may be happening A.M. too! Love P.M." (The album Paul mentions in the letter is The White Album.)

This lyric sheet was used and completed in Abby Road Studios for the song "Ob-La-Di, Ob-La-Da", which appears on The Beatles White Album released in 1968. The words to the song are written on the reverse side of a studio recording sheet in blue ink the hand of former Beatles' road manager and assistant, the late Mal Evans. The lyrics are also highlighted and penned in a black ink with additions, corrections, etc. by Paul McCcartney, who was putting the finishing touches on it before recording the song. It's likely that this very sheet was used during the session.

> MACLEN (MUSIC) LIMITED.
>
> RESOLUTION IN WRITING OF ALL THE DIRECTORS IN ACCORDANCE WITH THE COMPANY'S ARTICLES OF ASSOCIATION.
>
> Change of Secretary.
>
> IT IS RESOLVED that Moor House Secretaries Limited be and is hereby appointed Secretary of the Company with effect from December 13, 1968 in the place of Mr. B. F. Burns who submitted his resignation with effect from November 29, 1968.
>
> DATED this   day of   1969
>
> ....
> N. S. Aspinall.
>
> ....
> J. W. Lennon
>
> ....
> J. P. McCartney.

Maclen Music Limited document signed by Neil Aspinall, representing Apple, John Lennon and Paul McCartney in 1969.

The Beatles Looking Back: The Final Trip

Ken Mansfield, the former U.S. manager of the Beatles' Apple Records, promoted The Beatles on Capitol prior to being among the first on the Apple team. Starting with "Hey Jude," Mansfield played a crucial role in promoting The Beatles' music, as well as promoting other Apple acts such as Mary Hopkin, James Taylor, Jackie Lomax, and Badfinger.

Mansfield left Apple for MGM when John Lennon, George Harrison, and Ringo Starr appointed Allen Klein as The Beatles' manager in the spring of 1969, against Paul McCartney's wishes.

In 2018, Mansfield published his second memoir on his time with workiing with The Beatles titled, The Roof: The Beatles' Final Concert. In it, he talks about being there in person to see the last Beatles live performance on January 30, 1969. Ken passed away in 2022 at the age of 85.

This rare handwritten post card to Ken Mansfield from Paul McCartney is completely written in Paul's handwriting. As you see, he signed it humerously, "Love from Paul, Ron, Ive and Tony", aka Paul, John, George and Ringo.

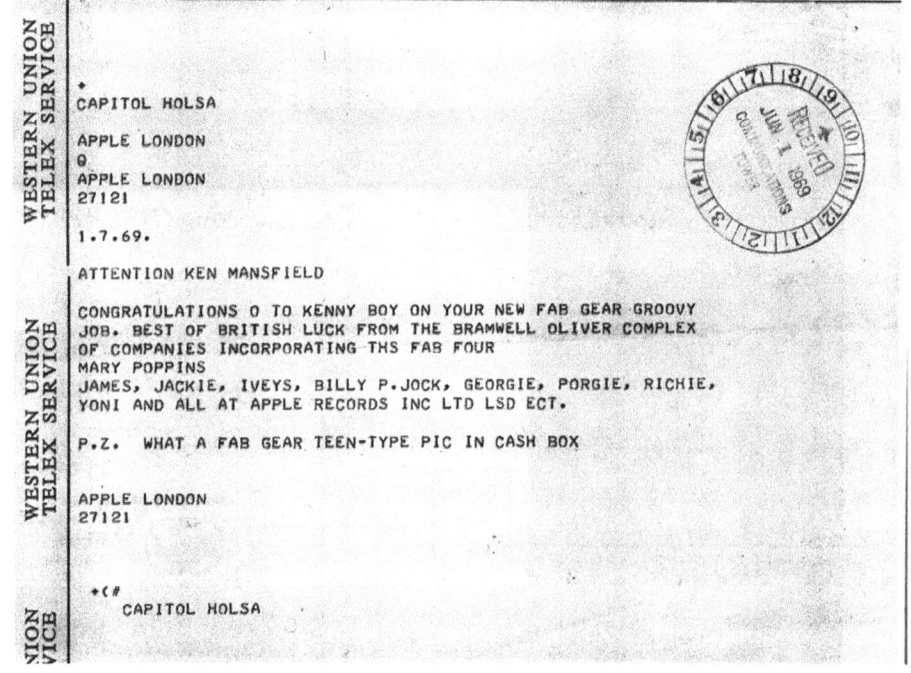

I looked deep into the archives and found nice and legible copies of this post card above along with a telegram from The Beatles to Ken, shown at the left. This was sent around the time The Beatles were recording their final album, Abbey Road.

The Beatles Looking Back: The Final Trip

A set of original art cels of all four Beatles' characters from their film Yellow Submarine in 1968.

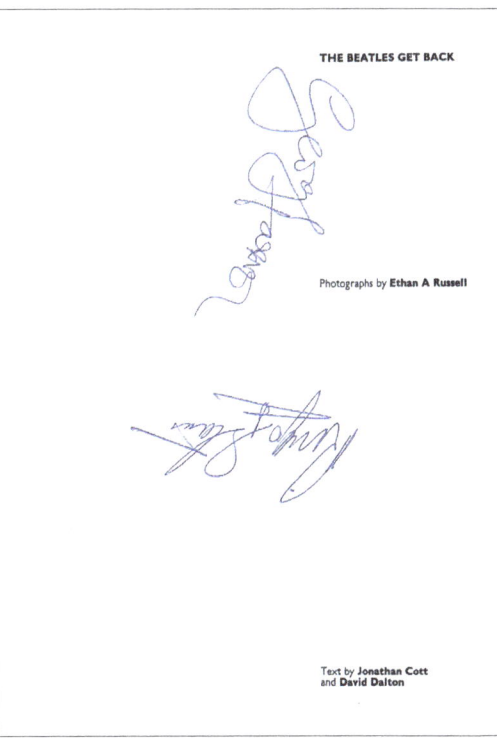

Get Back *book signed on the inside by George Harrison and Ringo Starr. These signatures were obtained right before the Beatles break up in April 1970. Quite rare.*

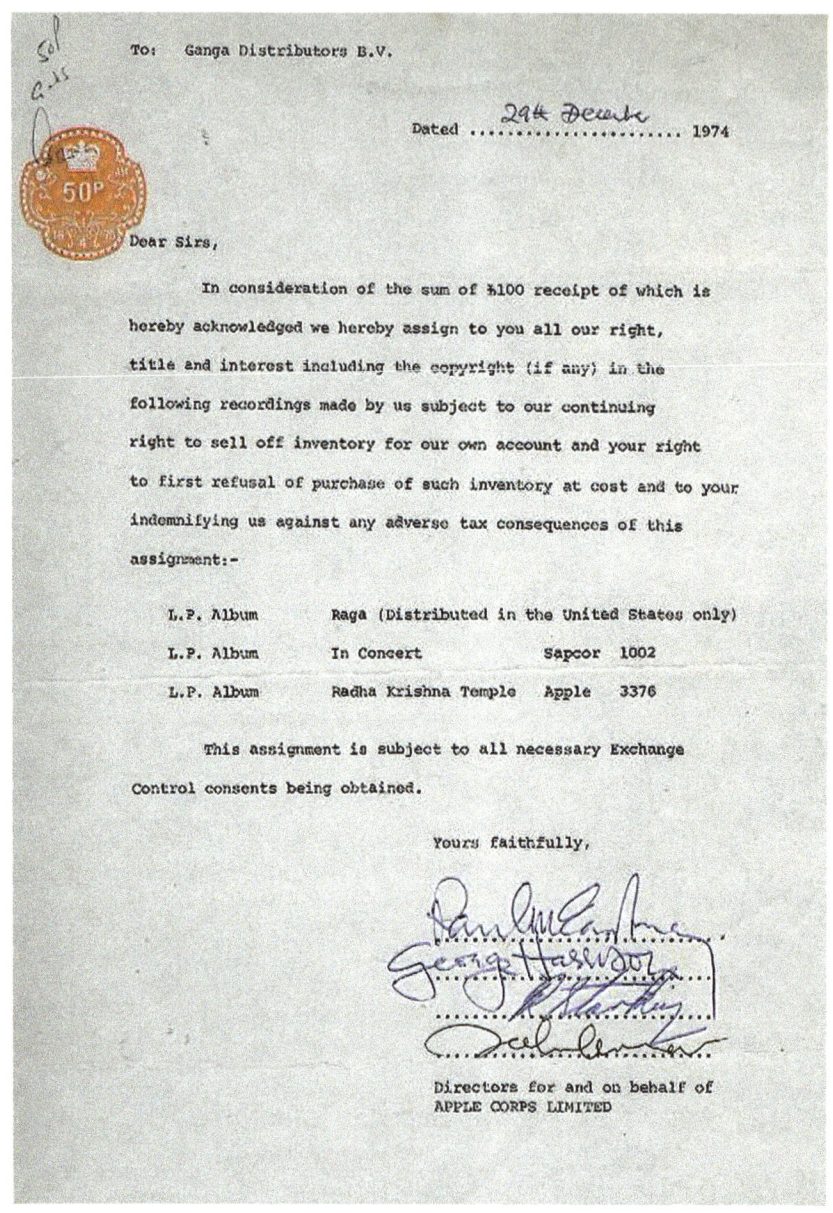

A contract regarding Apple album recordings of Raga *from the US,* In Concert *and* Radha Krishna Temple. *The contract was signed by all four Beatles as the directors of Apple on December 29, 1974.*

Consecutively numbered checks from National Westminster Bank Limited, made out to John Lennon on 25/3/75 and one to Paul McCartney on 24/3/75 and signed by both on each check as Directors of Maclen.

A sterling transfer form signed by John Lennon and Paul McCartney in 1976

The Beatles Looking Back: The Final Trip

Original unpublished 8x10 photos of The Beatles at their press conference in Cincinnati, Ohio in 1964. The photo was signed by all four members at various times in the mid to late 1970s, after the group's breakup. Very rare!

The Beatles Looking Back: The Final Trip

A unique 8x10 Capitol records promo photo featuring two images of The Beatles. What makes this truly rare is that each photo was signed twice by Lennon, McCartney, and Starr in the 1970s, post Beatles break up. I purchased this directly from the recipient of the signatures. He actually met George Harrison a few times, but he would not sign the photo for him. Harrison did sign other things though, including a picture sleeve that was signed by all four. Great item.

"The impact of the Beatles —
not only on rock & roll but on all of Western culture —
is simply incalculable …
[A]s personalities, they defined and incarnated '60s style:
smart, idealistic, playful, irreverent, eclectic….
[N]o group has so radically transformed the sound and significance
of rock & roll. …
[they] proved that rock & roll could embrace a limitless variety
of harmonies, structures, and sounds;
virtually every rock experiment has some precedent on Beatles record."

— Rolling Stone

John Lennon

"A dream you dream alone is only a dream.
A dream you dream together is reality."

— John Lennon

> 251. MENLOVE AVE
> WOOLTON
> LIVERPOOL 25
> LANCS.
>
> Dear Dawn,
>
> Thanks for your letter, glad you liked the show.
>
> For fan-club information, I can't tell you about opening a Stoke-on-Trent branch but suggest you get in touch with the Northern branch here in Liverpool and they can let you know all about it. The address is NEMS 12-14 Whitechapel
> Liverpool 1.
> Lancs.
>
> Thanks again — hope to be in Hanley again soon.
>
> Cheerio
> love
> John Lennon
> x

John Lennon's handwritten letter to a fan, sent from his Menlove Avenue address in 1962.

The Beatles Looking Back: The Final Trip

A very rare handwritten two-page letter from John Lennon to his friend Lindy Ness, along with the original envelope which Lennon addressed by hand. He also drew and wrote on the back as well (see page 87). This letter was written in August of 1962 addressed on the front and the back.

The Beatles Looking Back: The Final Trip

Don't be more sad if this letter isn't long enough but it's Thursday when I got up and I didn't find your letter till Wednesday evening 'cause I had not been to my place of residence for 2 days

"If you were the only girl in the world

— And I was a homosexual"

sung to the tune of God Help ye Merry Gents.

I'm falling asleep as I write and it's most peculiar in fact funny but I don't feel like larfing I feel sicks.

I hope this letter catches you before you leave Khrushcheviot and Sister Thingy.

Goodnight Lindy
(I'm in my pit with etc)
again Good god
love from
John
xxx
x

P.S. It's not a nice letter really I'm sorry.

goodnight SAD NESS
from

Lindy Ness
c/o Eric Laurås
LANGERSUND
NORWAY.

from J. Beatle,
sorry it's late
but betty late the nigger.

✝ S.W.A.L.C.

MEIN
GOTT!
(we say).

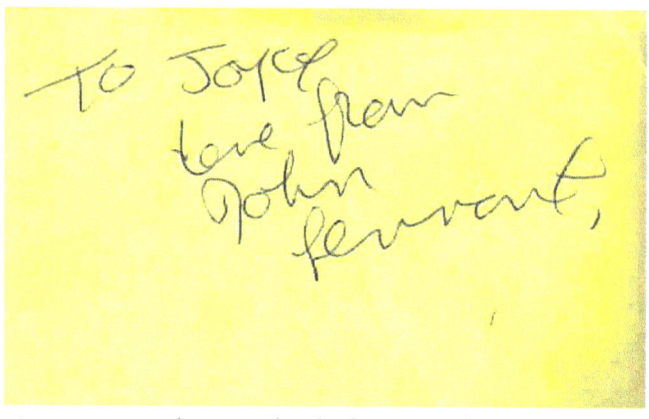

A small picture of John that has been cut out of a group photo. It is signed on the back, and the date and location (The Cavern) have been added.

A very nice early example of John Lennon's autograph dating from from late 1961 to early 1962.

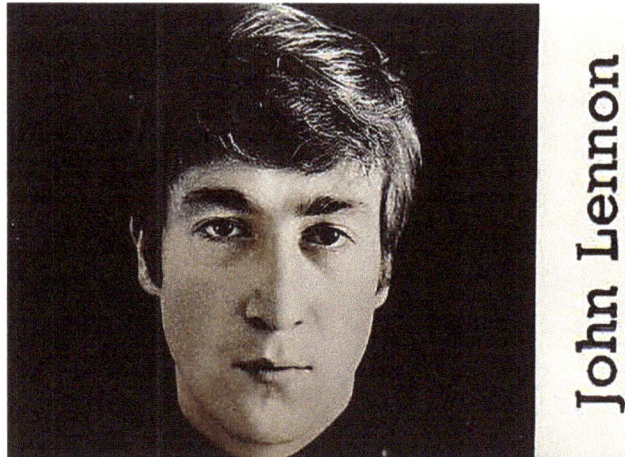

A John Lennon promo card signed nicely on the back by John in 1962 with German inscription above.

The Beatles Looking Back: The Final Trip

John Lennon Promo Card signed with inscription on the reverse from 1962.

This early 1963 photo of John Lennon is his image on television and was taken when a he was featured on a television show. It is signed on the back with inscription: "Love to Georgia from John Lennon xxx." This was a clever way to obtain his photo, and then to ask him to sign it later was genuis!

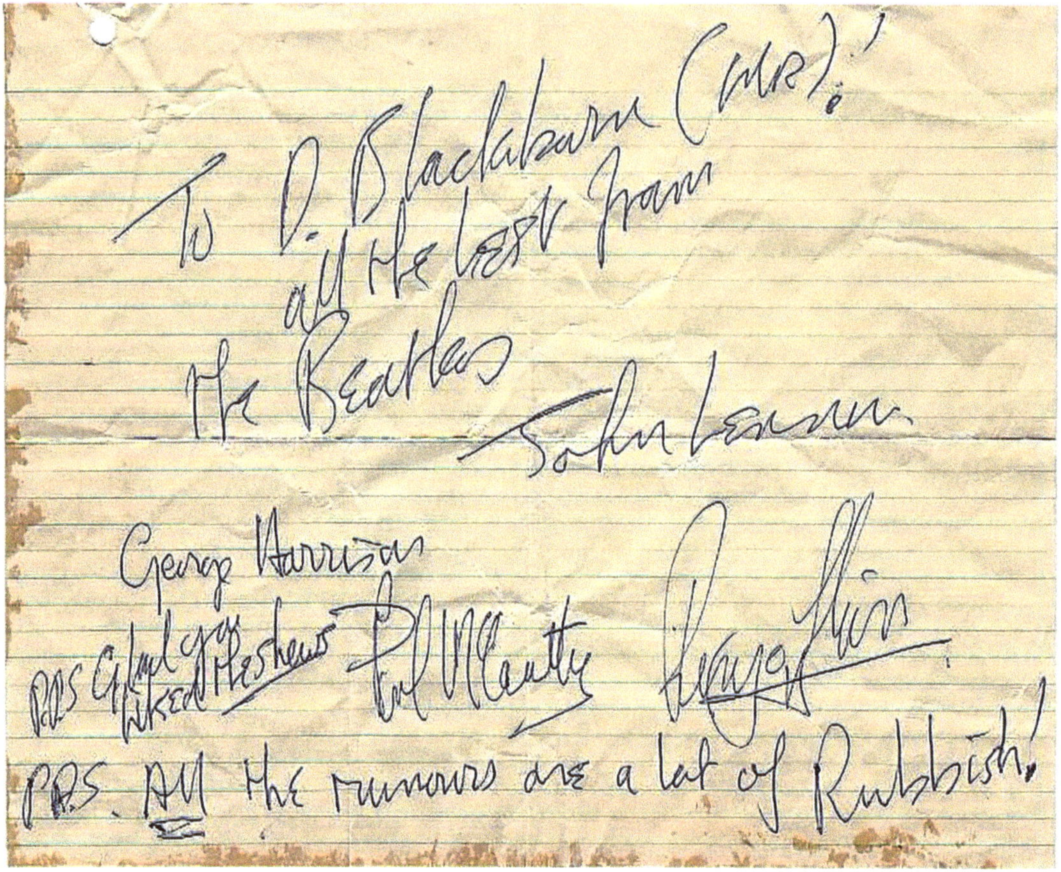

The Beatles Looking Back: The Final Trip

This is a unique John Lennon signed and inscribed note to D. Blackburn. What makes this note special is that all the writing is in Lennon's hand, including him signing for the other three Beatles. There have only been a few times where an individual Beatle signed for the other three, and this is a perfect example.

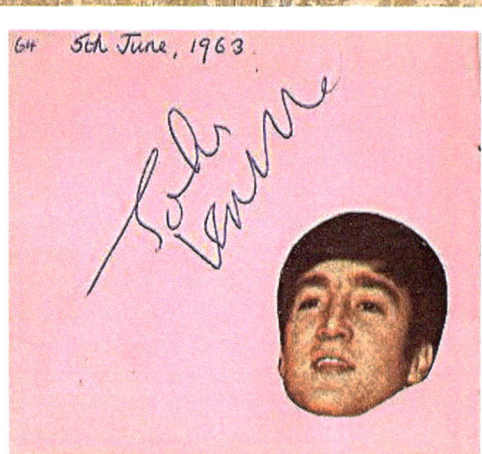

An autograph book page signed by John Lennon on June 5, 1963.

 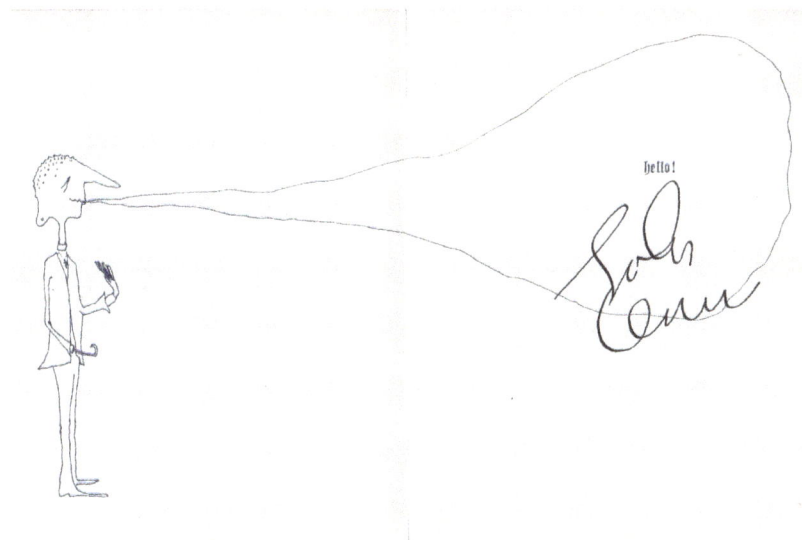

In His Own Write book by John Lennon has been signed on one of his drawings inside the book, and the title page has been signed by with Ringo Starr, with a dedication to Paula, lower right.

 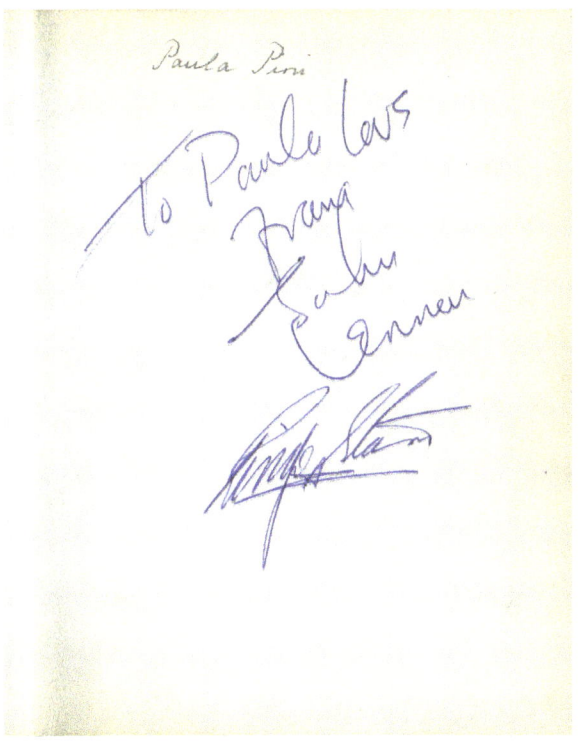

This picture folder from 1964 features a candid photo of John. He signed it: "To Angela Love John Lennon".

The Beatles Looking Back: The Final Trip

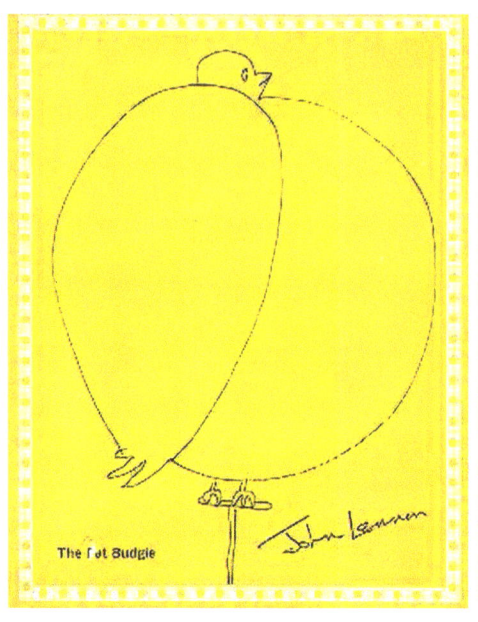

The Beatles were major supporters of Oxfam, especially John, and that continued past the days of The Beatleas. The card, The Fat Budgie (Lennon's Artwork), was a Christmas card sent to his family: Norman (Uncle), Julia and Jackey with all notations and inscription and signed: John, Cyn (his wife Cynthia, who started to sign his last name but changed the L to a C) and Julian xxx (his son). A very rare item around the holiday season.

This ticket for the 1964 Foyle's Luncheon, which took place at The Dorchester Hotel, is signed on the back by attendees John Lennon and singer Helen Shapiro. John was there to promote and sign his book *In His Own Write*.

The Beatles Looking Back: The Final Trip

This candid photograph of Ringo, taken while he was filming a scene for A Hard Day's Night, *was signed on the back by John Lennon in 1964.*

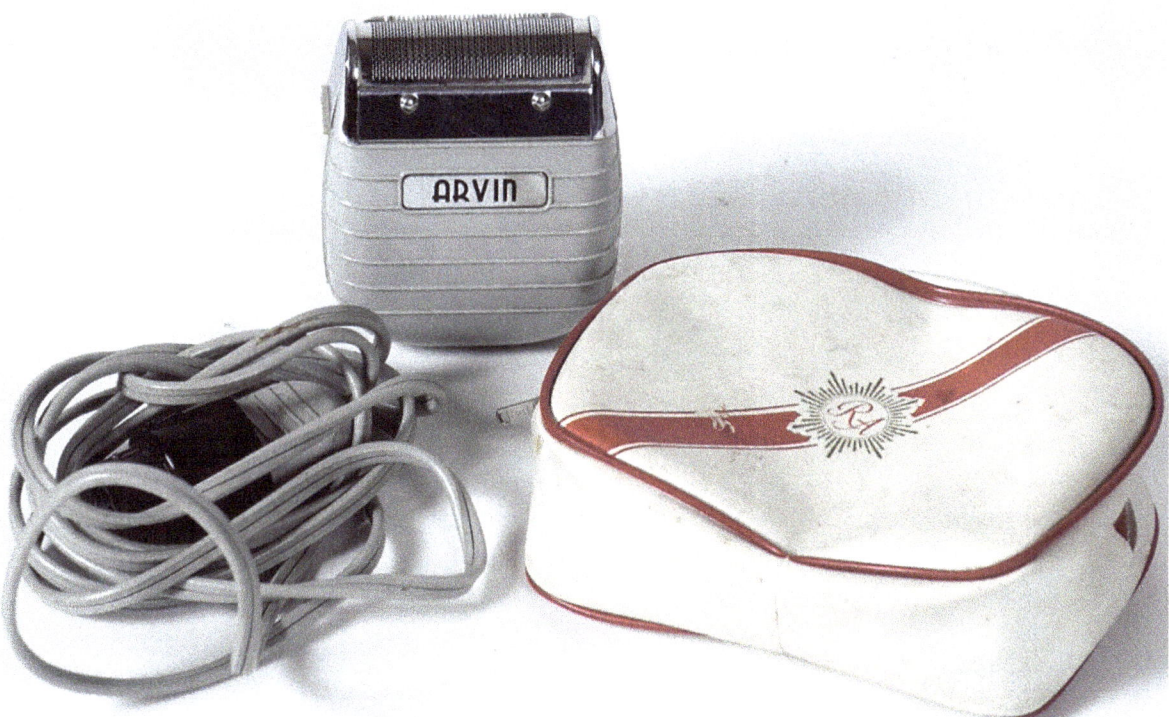

John Lennon's personally owned travel razor with case that he used during The Beatles tour years. This item was obtained from John's housekeeper, Dot Jarlett. She was employed by the Lennons in the 1960s and John her many items over the years.

The Beatles Looking Back: The Final Trip

This television guide from Holland was signed on the front and back by John Lennon. He also added his own comic renderings in ball point pen on each of his bandmates' faces and his own. This piece was obtained while The Beatles were on tour and includes a picture of John holding television guide before he signed it. Below is a detailed letter from the recipient of this item.

The Beatles in Holland for the VARA Television Network

It's June 1964 and I'm the Art Director of the VARA, a television and radio network in Hilversum. When news arrives that The Beatles are going to play in Holland as well, the VARA wastes no time in contracting them for a television spot. The session is to take place in Treslong, a large hall in Hillegom between Haarlem and The Hague.

The editor of the Radio-TV guide comes up with a competition for young readers of the magazine: make your own drawing of The Beatles!
A photo portrait of The Beatles will adorn the cover of the guide.

On the day of the TV shoot I'm in Hillegom with several other radio-TV magazines, all of them of course wanting The Beatles for their front covers as well. Herman Stok, the presenter of the radio programme "Tijd for Teenagers" (Time for Teenagers) is there too.
Rehearsals are busily underway and the famous television presenter Berend Boudewijn holds several interviews with John, Paul, George and Jimmie in their dressing room - Ringo's not there this time.

After the interviews have taken place I ask the three real Beatles and Ringos'stand-in Jimmie Nichols if they could sign the cover of the magazine for me. They all sign it and one of them even writes an address down and a few names of people that I might want to look up later in London. John grabs the other magazine, scribbles moustaches and glasses on each of the portraits and signs it.

The television session is totally playback: A Hard Days Night, the opening song, was then right at the top of the charts. The legendary boat trip through the canals of Amsterdam that the "Fab Four" made later that day left a massive impression on the lads, even after the Beatlemania madness they had already experienced prior to Amsterdam. All of the bridges in the city were jam-packed with people throwing flowers at them, many of them jumping into the canal to get closer to their idols. It was amazing!

An interesting piece of pop trivia from that legendary canal trip is that John's attention was caught by a cape someone was wearing on the side of the canal as their boat passed. That cape would later serve as a prototype model for their outfits in the film A Hard Days Night (See Beatles Anthology, page 139).

The Beatles Looking Back: The Final Trip

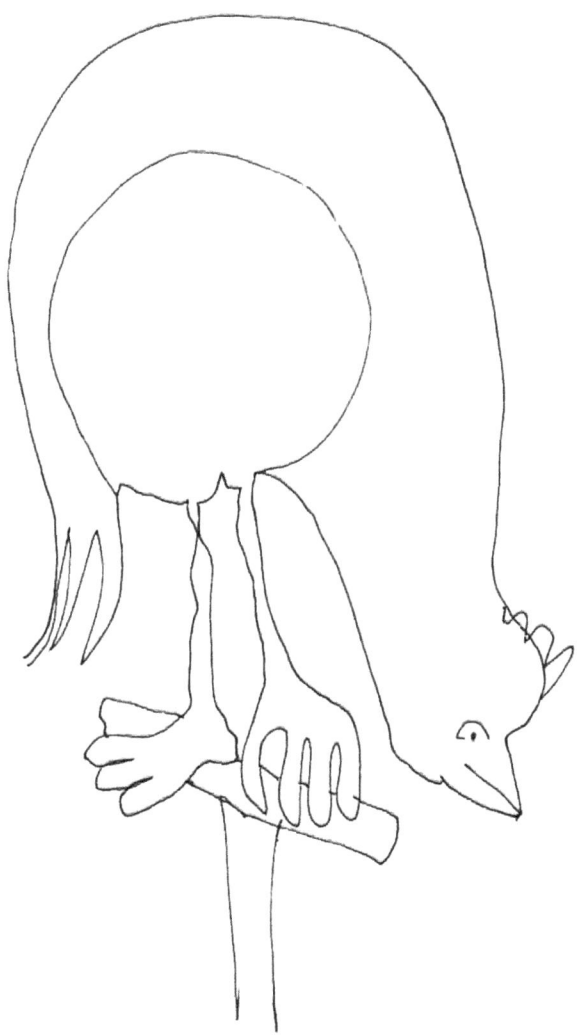

Original drawing by John Lennon titled "Bird on a Perch" derived from his book A Spanierd in the Works.

John Lennon's second book, A Spaniard in the Works, *was released in 1965. John has signed on the inside cover page.*

A nice John Lennon signature on Charlton Tower (London) hotel stationery, annotated at the top by the recipient: 19/12/63.

John Lennon's personally owned and used movie camera from the 1960s. A note from Cynthia Lennon accompanies this piece, verifying its provenience.

John Lennon signed this picture of him that appeared in Beatles Monthly *magazine in 1965.*

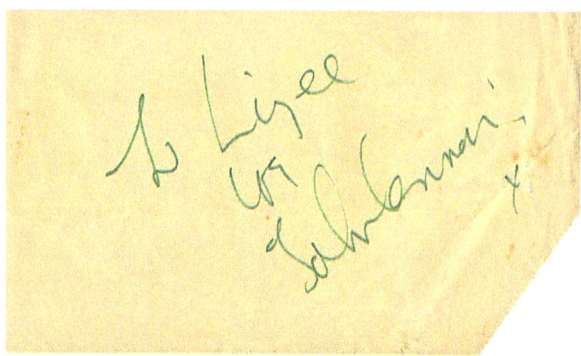

Apple Scruff girl Lizzie Bravo met with The Beatles and received their autographs on many occasions. This photo is a nicely signed on a page that was dedicated: "To Lizzee Love John Lennon" came from her collection. The magazine photo (at left) of John and Cynthia Lennon that was signed by John is also from her collection.

This candid photograph of John at his home in 1967 was signed by John on the front, lightly, and the boldly on the other side.

This candid Polaroid photo of John Lennon with Ringo Starr in the background was signed in black ball point pen by Lennon in 1967.

A *Magical Mystery Tour* EP signed by John Lennon in the centerfold from 1967.

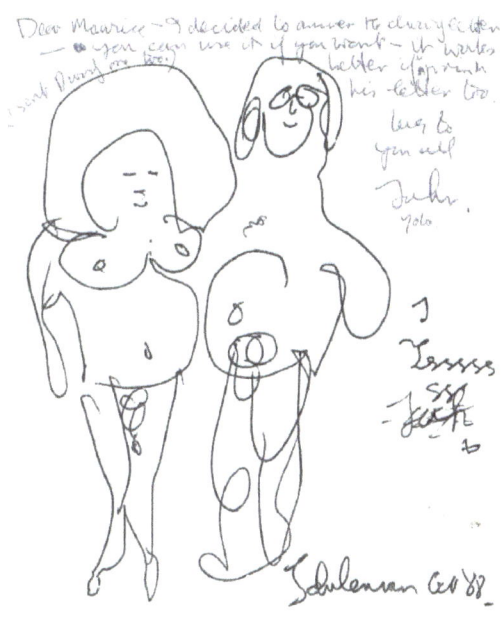

A handwritten and signed note to a journalist who had written a story about John. Lennon wrote it on a copy of a drawing of he and Yoko from 1968.

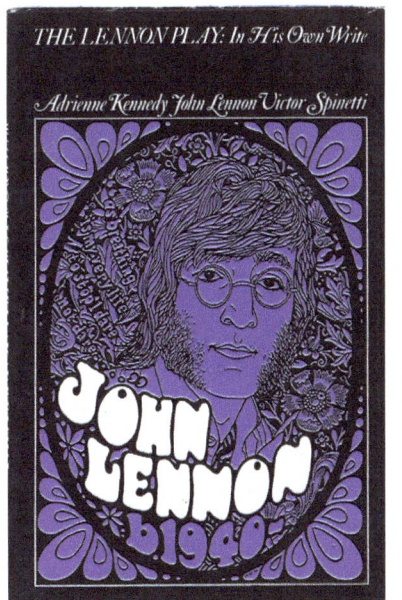

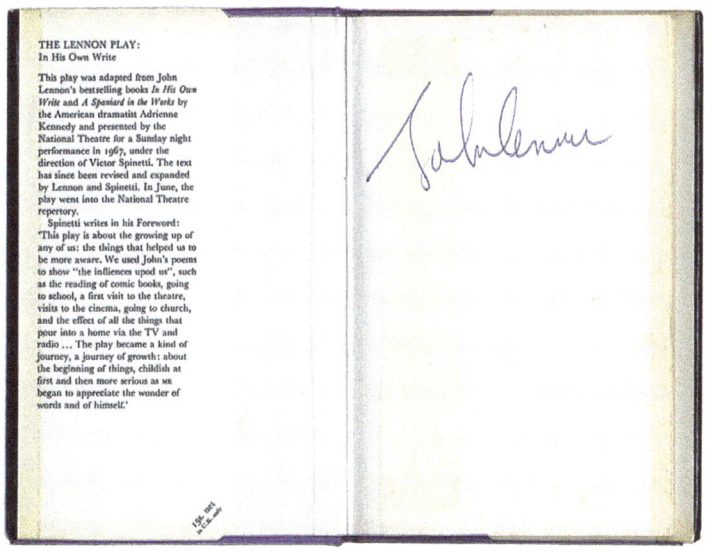

This first edition of The Lennon Play: In His Own Write, *written by Adrienne Kennedy, John Lennon and Victor Spinetti, was signed on the inside by Lennon in 1968. This is the only signed copy of the first edition that has surfaced to date. The unsigned book is also quite difficult to find.*

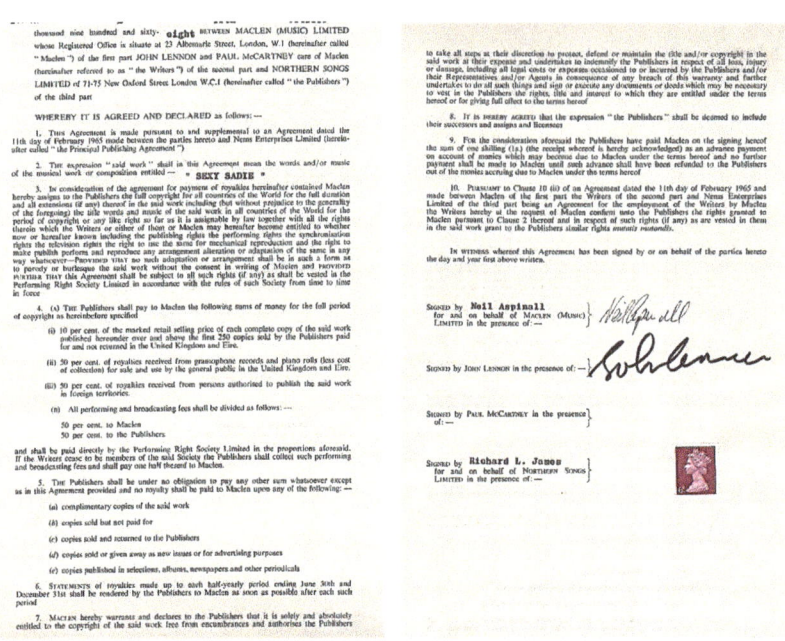

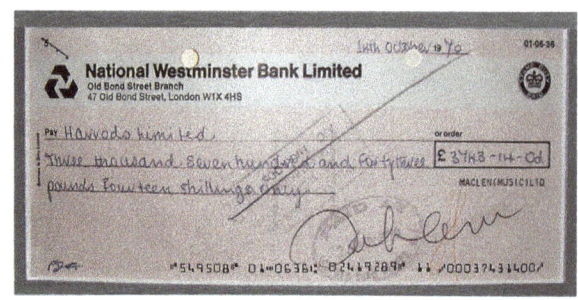

This National Westminster Bank Limited check was filled out in another person's handwriting and signed by John. It is dated October 14, 1970.

This is a publishing agreement from 1968 regarding The Beatles' song "Sexy Sadie" from The White Album. It is *signed on the back by John Lennon and Neil Aspinall on behalf of Maclen Music.*

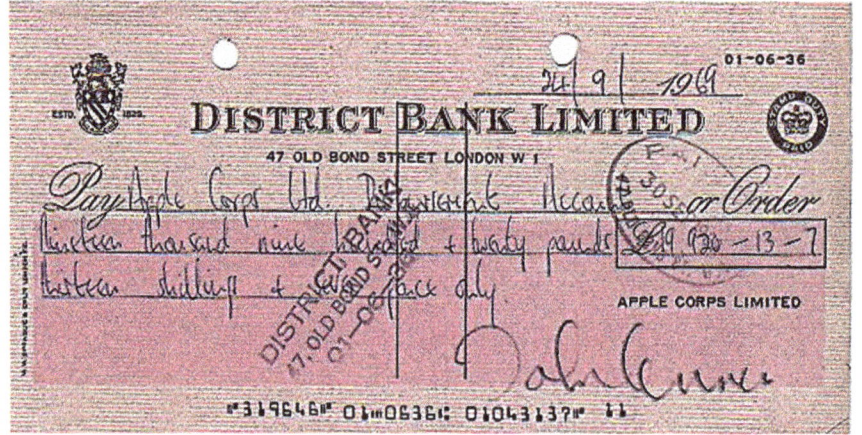

This District Bank Limited check is made out in another person's handwriting to Apple Corp Ltd. and signed by John Lennon. The date on the check is September 24, 1969.

The Beatles Looking Back: The Final Trip

```
Letter of Provenance              May 17, 1993
John Lennon's Running Suit

After my divorce from Yoko Ono in 1969, she and John Lennon stayed with
me and my daughter Kyoko at my farmhouse in Denmark for nearly a month
in January, 1970.  During this time we were trying to develop our
friendship, and we spent a lot of time relaxing around the house, making
vegetarian meals together, playing music and singing.

During the visit, John and Yoko wore identical Danish running suits
almost all the time.  John's two suits were navy blue, while Yoko's were
red.  This suit is one of those worn by John.  It has a white zipper and
a jacket that zips all the way up the front to a high-standing collar
(no hood), and one outside zippered pocket.  The pants have an elastic
waist, one inside pocket, zippers at the ankles, and stirrups.  The suit
was made by HF Dragten of Denmark.

During this visit, the Lennons decided to have their long, trademark
hair cut off, as a symbol of beginning the new decade of the 70's.  At
the time this action shocked a great many people, who viewed long hair
as an integral part of people involved in the counterculture.  The
press, which had followed the Lennons to Denmark, were adamant about
photographing them with their new crewcuts.  Photographers spent long
days standing in the snow and bitter cold in the driveway of my
farmhouse.

In order to gain some peace, I took the first photographs of the Lennons
with short hair.  They are wearing their running suits in the pictures.
I was later told that the photographer to whom I gave the film sold the
first prints to the press for $10,000.

Sincerely yours,

Tony Cox

Tony Cox
```

John Lennon and Yoko Ono planned a vacation to Denmark to see Yoko's daughter Kyoko and Yoko's ex-husband, Tony Cox, and his wife in 1970. While there, John had two jogging suits made. The one pictured above is the suit John used on more than one occasion. Tony Cox shot the very first pictures of John and Yoko wearing the jogging suits after they cut off all their hair for charity. Included with the suit is a letter from Cox confirming the suit was owned and worn by Lennon. The other suit came up for auction several years ago, but that suit was never worn by Lennon.

The Beatles Looking Back: The Final Trip

HISTORY OF AUTOGRAPHS OF JOHN LENNON, YOKO ONO & KYOKO

John, Yoko and Kyoto were holidaying in Durness in the North West of Sutherland in the Highlands of Scotland where John had relatives.

On their way home they unfortunately had a car accident and were taken to the nearest hospital which was the Lawson Memorial Hospital in Golspie in East Sutherland.

My aunt was a nurse in the hospital and got the signatures for me.

I believe this was in 1969 and I have had the autographs since then.

Janette Carrison

Autographed pages of John Lennon, Yoko Ono Lennon, Kyoko (Yoko's daughter) and Julian (John's son). The signatures were obtained at the hospital where John and family were treated for injuries received in a car accident. The nurse who checked them in was given the autographs. This is one of two sets to surface that were signed at the hospital that day.

The Beatles Looking Back: The Final Trip

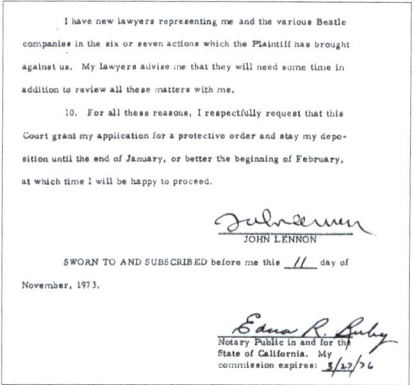

John Lennon and Yoko Ono's contract with Geraldo Rivera for their famous One to One concert at Madison Square Garden.

These are two of the five pages of John Lennon's lawsuit to end his association with ABKC (Allen Klein) from 1973. What makes this document so historical is that Lennon, Harrison, and Starr agreed to Klein managing The Beatles' business affairs, but McCartney did not. This was the beginning of the rift between band members that eventually led to the The Beatles breakup on April 10, 1970 when McCartney he would no longer be a part of the group.

The Beatles Looking Back: The Final Trip

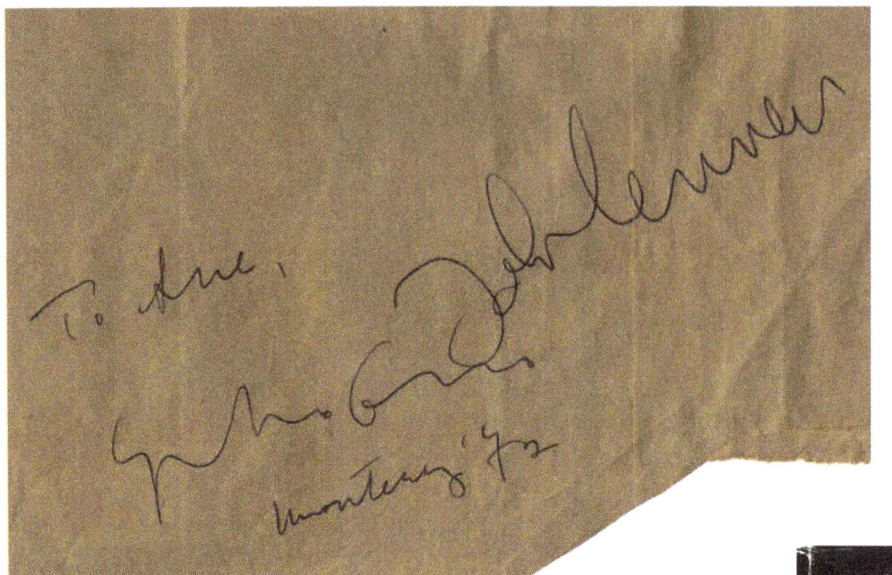

This is torn piece of department store bag is signed by John Lennon and Yoko Ono. It is also dedicated and dated by Yoko: Monterey '72. I guess this proves that you never know what celebrities will sign.

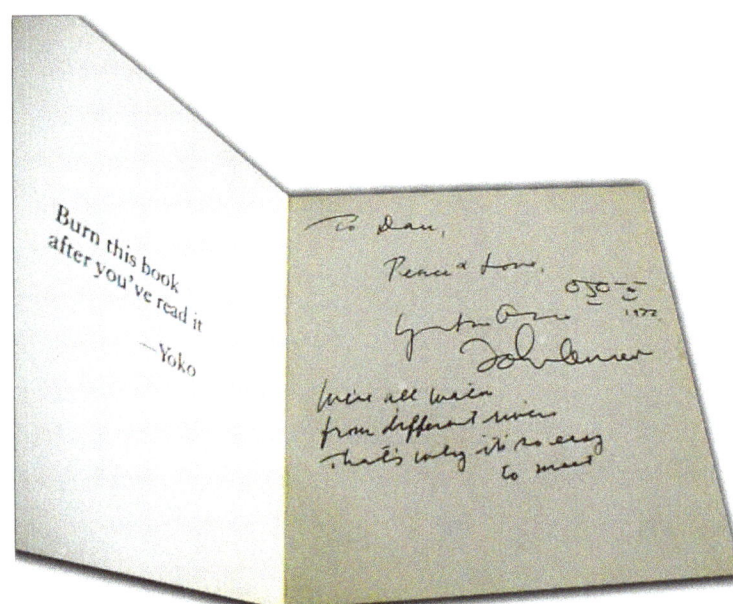

A rarer version of Grapefruit, the book *by Yoko Ono, with black and white cover from 1971. It is signed on on the inside first page by Yoko Ono with a dedication and partial lyrics to "We're All Water" by Yoko . John Lennon has signed the book as well, adding he and Yoko's face doodle and dated it 1972.*

Apple

MEMORANDUM

To: Date: Nov: ?

From: Subject:

Dear Les and family,

As you know we seem to be living half our lives abroad these days, and it's crazy to keep a large staff, as we need people here – right? You've been a good lad over the years and faithful – for which I thank you. I know you've spoken to Peter Howard and Dan about leaving – and I hope the arrangements suit you,

See you some day

all the best from

John & Yoko

P.S. if there's anything you want to say to us, call May at ABKCO; if you need a reference – tell us what you need.

P.P.S. say goodbye to your wife & the kids. xxx

John's nice handwritten letter on Apple Memorandum stationery, November 1973.

John Lennon signed his *Walls and Bridges* album cover and dedicated it to the children of the recipient. He also added a face doodle and another small drawing, and dated it 74.

The Beatles Looking Back: The Final Trip

I was fortunate enough to have another Wall and Bridges *album signed by John Lennon in 1974. He dedicated this one to the children of the recipient as well. This time though, besides his his face doodle, he added two small drawings. Incredible!*

The Beatles Looking Back: The Final Trip

A original A Hard Days Night preview ticket signed on the front by John Lennon, who has added a face doodle and dated it 74.

A master production tape from 1974 that contains a John Lennon interview done over the phone from New York for a Dallas radio station. This interview, filled with interesting content, was only ever copied onto one CD, which accompanies the tape.

The release of John Lennon's Walls and Bridges album was accompanied by an advertising campaign, created by Lennon, called "Listen To This..." (matchbook, button, photo, sticker, ad, poster, T-shirt, etc.). The backs of 500 New York City buses were even plastered with the slogan "Listen To This Bus". This matchbook was signed on the inside cover by John, who really wanted this album to be successful. It was, and includes several memorable songs.

A record award from 93KHJ radio for the song "Whatever Gets You Through The Night" that achieved #1 status in 1974.

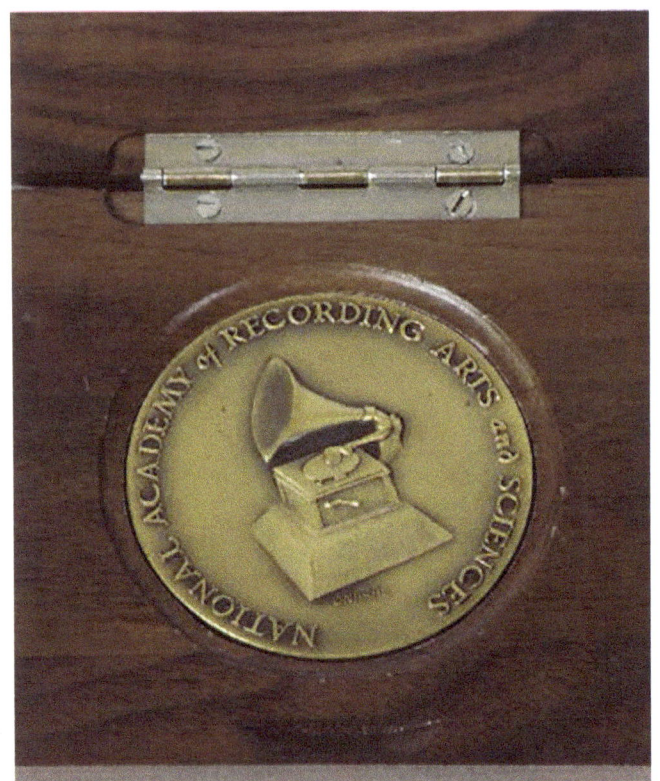

John Lennon's Grammy presentation medal encased in a wooden box. This was given to John for appearing on the 1975 Grammy Awards. John donated this award to an Indiana charity and I later purchased it from them.

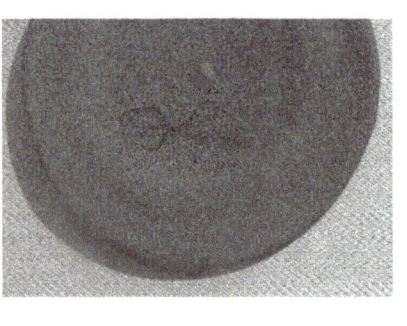

John Lennon's personally owned, worn and signed black beret. (The image was lightened and converted to black and white to show the signature.) John can be seen wearing this beret at the 1975 Grammy Awards, where he was a presenter.

The Beatles Looking Back: The Final Trip

A rare stage play handbill for Sgt. Pepper On the Road (A Rock Spectacle), *signed on the front by John Lennon in 1974, along with the original flyer.*

HELPING HAND MARATHON

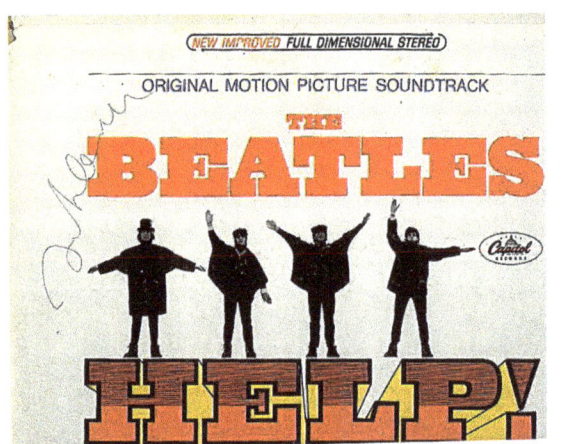
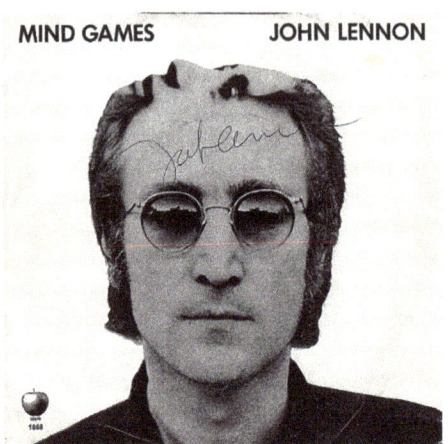

In May of 1975, John Lennon was invited to attend The Helping Hand Marathon in Philadelphia, Pa., by Larry Kane, an old friend from The Beatles days. While there, John even appeared on TV as a weatherman exhibiting his typical humor. He really gave his time and support to the event all weekend by signing autographs for a charitable contribution. He even signed his latest album, *Rock and Roll*, as well as 45 picture sleeves of "Mind Games." John was open to signnig anything fans set in front of him. Above is a sampling of the items I owned that were signed at this event.

HELPING HAND MARATHON (CONTINUED)

ALBUM
Signed on:
Sat. May. 17, 1975
5/17/75
At WPLJ-Phila.

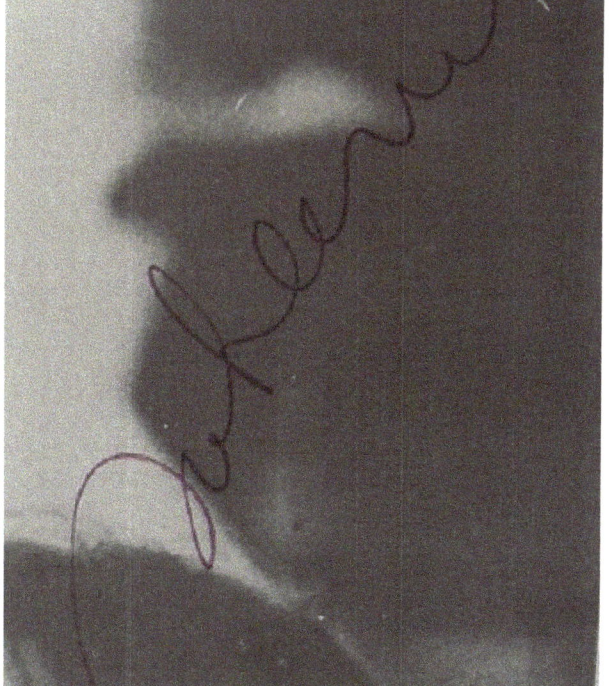

HELPING HAND MARATHON (CONTINUED)

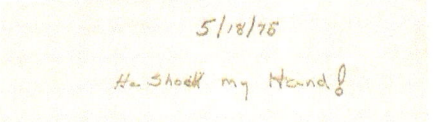

5/18/75
He Shook my Hand!

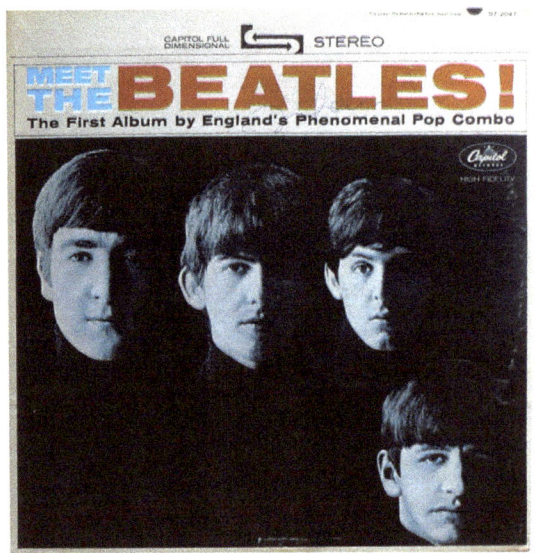

The Beatles Looking Back: The Final Trip

John Lennon's personally owned and worn "Home" shirt accompanied by a picture of John wearing the shirt in the studio in 1975.

```
LENNON MUSIC
1370 AVENUE OF THE AMERICAS                july 31.75.
NEW YORK, NEW YORK 10019
212-586-6444
TELEX: 148315
```

Dear Whoever,

      You are now the proud owner of a rather unique set of Lennon lithographs.Having caused a scandal on both sides of the Atlantic, a few rare sets became even rarer by being spoiled or improved by the mighty Hudson...which somehow managed to seep into the basement of John and Yokos' Soho loft!They were originally printed in the late Avante Guarde,(a now defunct mag.)A limited number were sold throughout the world. (I'VE FORGOTTEN HOW MANY).Rumour has it that Dali bought a set...he'll do anything to get in the newspapers!

      love to the owner,

      may all your children be human!

    j.l.

A very cool typewritten and signed letter by John Lennon from 1975. He has also added a face doodle and dated 75 below his signature. Again, I dug deep into my archives and found a really nice copy of this because I wanted to share this with you. The subject of the letter was the Bag One lithographs that John had signed years earlier.

An 8x10 promotional photo of John Lennon's Rock and Roll *album released in 1975. John is pictured in Hamburg in 1961, photographed by Jurgen Vollmer. John has signed the photo at the botton. I met Jurgen Vollmer in 1997 at Planet Hollywood in Indianapolis while he was there promoting his book* Vollmer from Hamburg to Hollywood, *and he agreed to sign the photo at the top.*

This candid 7x9 black and white wire photo of John and Yoko coming out of The Dakota is signed by John Lennon, who added a face doodle and dated it 76 (even though it looks like 70). I obtained this signed photo from a New York collector who met all of The Beatles over the years and was given several autographs by each of them at various locations.

The Beatles Looking Back: The Final Trip

A signed playbill for the Merce Cunningham Dance performance in New York, which John and Yoko attended in 1977. A picture of John signing his autograph accompanies the playbill.

A New York Count Commercial code financing statement signed by John Lennon and Yoko Ono in the late 1970s.

The Beatles Looking Back: The Final Trip

Here, you see John Lennon's autograph on a 13"x16" envelope-type shopping bag from Japan. The signature was obtained in person during the summer of 1979, during John's final trip to Japan with Yoko and Sean. He has also added a face doodle of himself and dated it 79. At the bottom the recipient added 8/9/79.

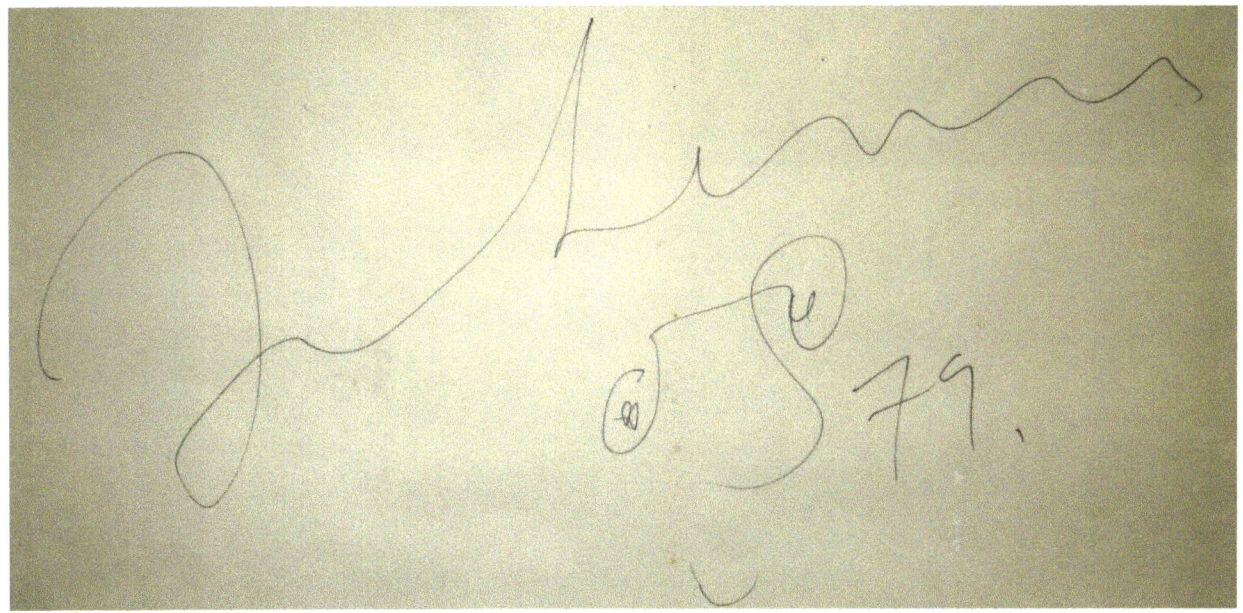

119

The Beatles Looking Back: The Final Trip

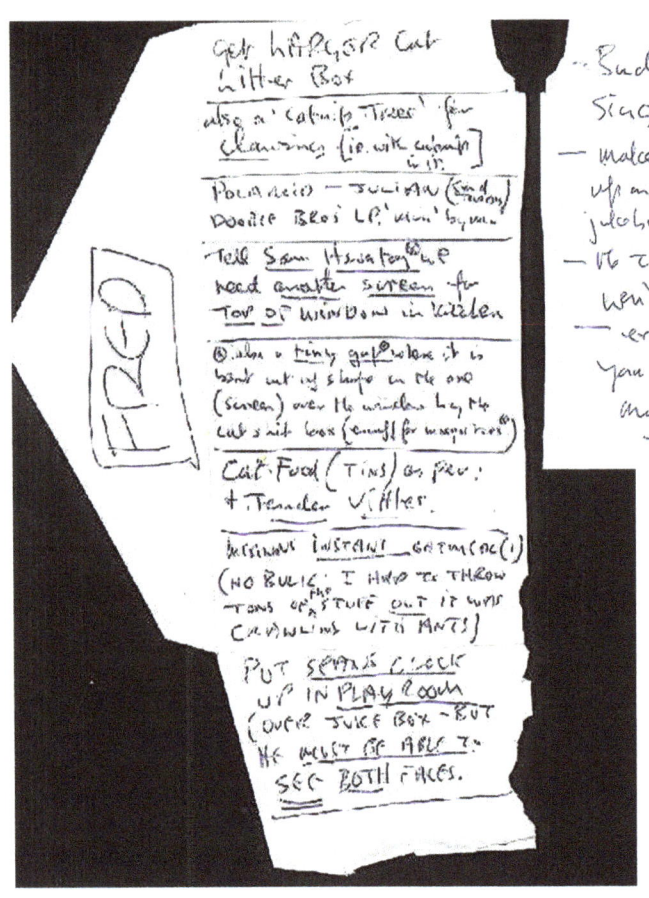

A handwritten "to do" list for John's assistant and friend, Fred Seaman, written on both sides of an envelope in 1980.

A handwritten front and back "to do" list written by John Lennon from the late 1970s. He has initialed at the bottom L.

The Beatles Looking Back: The Final Trip

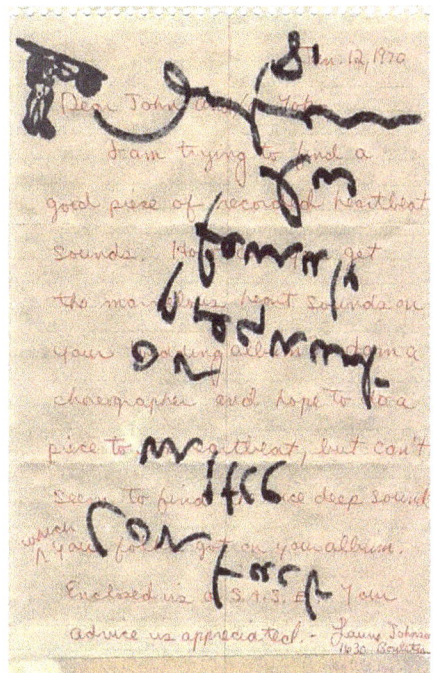 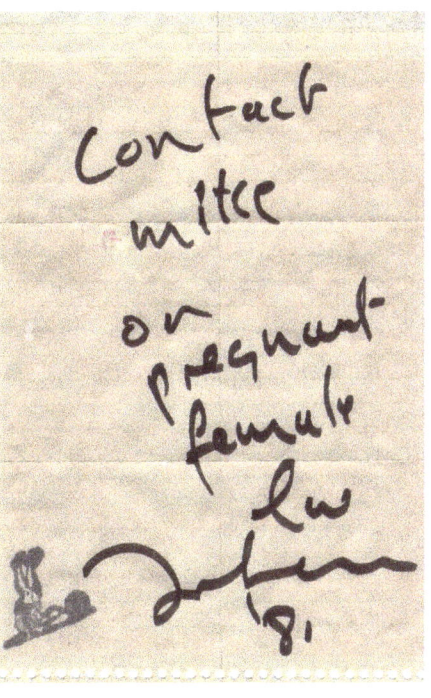

A fan wrote to John Lennon and Yoko on January 12, 1970, requesting recordings of a heartbeat sound and asking if will be on their next album etc. Ten years later, John answered her letter, saying, "Contact Mike on pregnant female love J lennon 80," and drew a doodle of a pregnant woman on her back with her feet up. I am glad she parted with the letter and it was great to have it in my collection. I can't believe John actually answered her after ten years!

A really nice post card addressed to Sam Green (who was in the arts and friends with the Lennons) in New York. It was handwritten by John and initialed J+Y with added face doodles of John and Yoko.

This is a handwritten postcard to Rosa Lopez and family from 1979, wishing them a "Merry Xmas" and "Happy 80s". Rosa was John and Yoko's maid at the Dakota from 1973–1980.

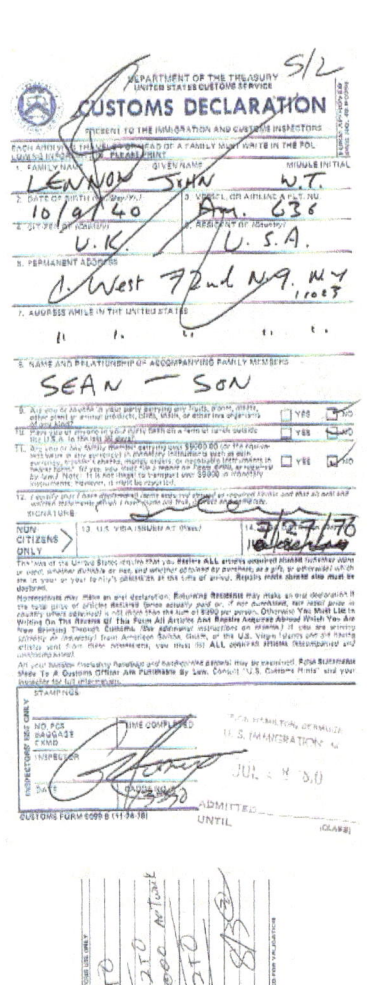
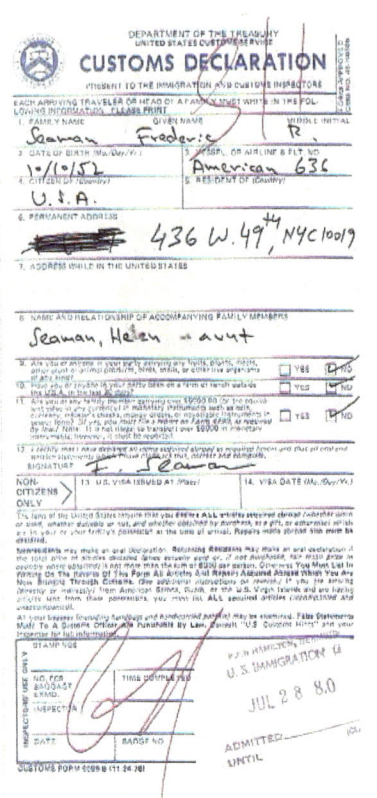
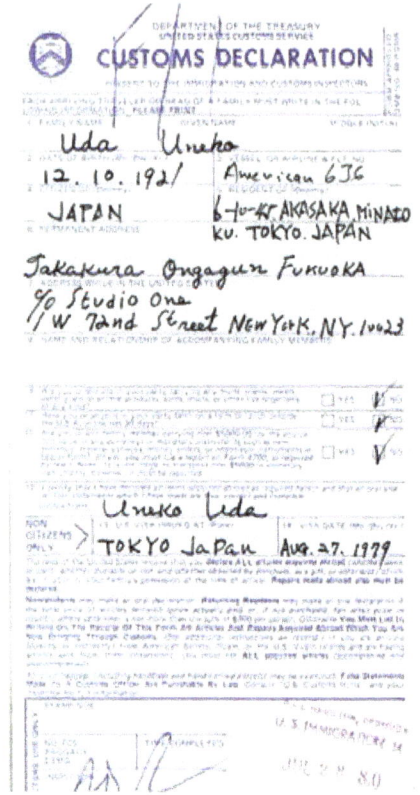
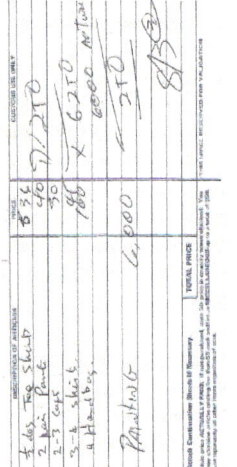
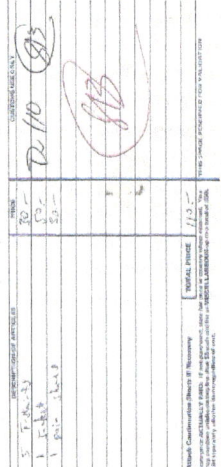

Customs declaration forms for John Lennon and his assistant, Fred Seamon. This was the time when John, Sean, Fred and Sean's guardian, Uda, went to Bermuda and sailed The Megan Jaye. They had to fill out and sign these forms for customs upon their return on July 28, 1980.

The Beatles Looking Back: The Final Trip

The Megan Jaye's logbook with artwork by John Lennon and signature by John in 1980. This book has been featured in news and magazine articles over the last several years. Included are the Customs declaration forms for John and Fred Seaman, who went on the trip to Bermuda.

The Beatles Looking Back: The Final Trip

John Lennon and Yoko Ono's Double Fantasy *album cover signed on the back and dedicated "To Cathy Love John Lennon". John signed only a hanful of these for when the album was released in mid-November of 1980, mainly for promotions, friends, etc. so finding one is rare.*

John was very good at answering fan mail and autograph requests late in his career. The recipient sent a self-addressed, stamped envelope to John at the Dakota, and he politely answered and signed this card "Love John Lennon" with one of his famous face doodles and dated it 80. What makes this truly rare (and sad) is the recipient received the autograph in the mail on December 9, 1980, the day after John was murdered.

John Lennon and Yoko Ono promotional 16x20 color prints matted and distributed by Polydor Records for the posthumous release of Milk and Honey *in 1983.*

The Beatles Looking Back: The Final Trip

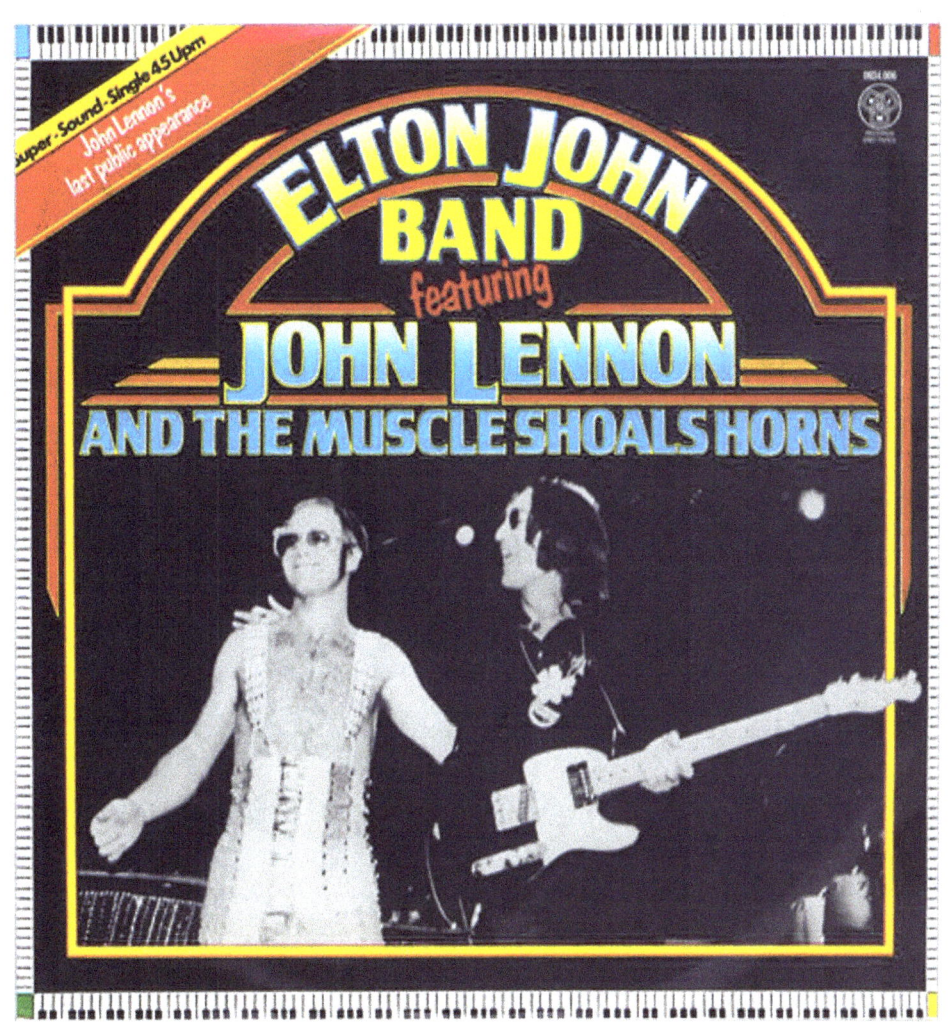

Dr. Winston O'Boogie and the Rocketman

"I remember being at school and my friend Michael Johnson came with a 45 and said, 'I've just heard this band, they're gonna be the biggest band in the world,' and it was 'Love Me Do'.
I listened to and said, 'It's not bad, it's not bad'.
I couldn't see that they would be the biggest band in the world, and he turned out to be right ... he spotted them a mile off."

— Elton John

(from 2022 Far Out Magazine *interview*)

The Beatles Looking Back: The Final Trip

JOHN LENNON'S LAST CONCERT APPEARANCE

DR. WINSTON O' BOOGIE AND THE ROCKETMAN

On Thanksgiving night, November 28th 1974, during Elton John's encore at Madison Square Garden, he was joined on stage by John Lennon, who performed a few numbers with Elton and the band. This magical night also reunited John with Yoko.

The following are items I collected from this event and once owned. They included the original newspaper concert review from the *New York Times*, the actual set list with the changes to support John's appearance, the stage costume Elton wore that night (which was on display for two years at The Rock and Roll Hall of Fame Museum in Cleveland, Ohio and is shown on the next page), and a dollar bill signed by both John Lennon and Elton John obtained after the concert when the entire entourage went to a bar. The bartender there was the recipient of the autographs, and John Lennon himself gave it to him. This historical event was John Lennon's last concert appearance.

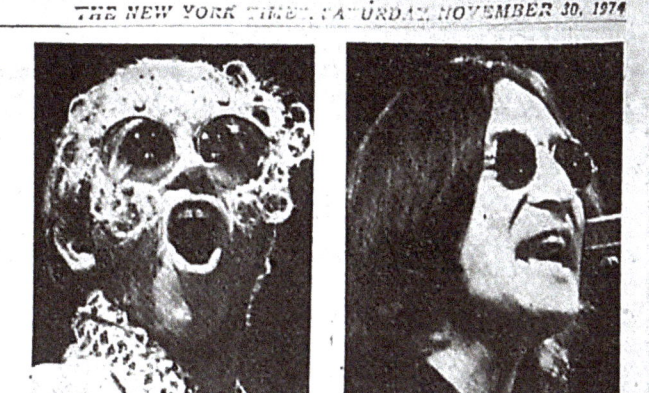

Elton John, left, and John Lennon at the Garden

Pop Music: Elton John at the Garden

But when Mr. Lennon came on, the Garden was transformed. Not that the crowd hadn't given every indication of loving Mr. John and his music. But with Mr. Lennon, there was an electricity that sparked through the crowd long after Mr. Lennon had left the stage.

The two men sang three songs together: Mr. Lennon's current single, "Whatever Gets You Through the Night" as a simultaneously sung duet, the Beatles' "Lucy in the Sky With Diamonds" (Mr. John's current single), with Mr. John singing the verses and Mr. Lennon and the audience joining in for the choruses, and, in another duet, the early Beatles song "I Saw Her Standing There," which Mr. Lennon introduced as being by "an old fiancé of mine called Paul."

Far left, Elton John's costume from the Madison Square Garden concert, shown when it was on display at The Rock and Roll Hall of Fame in Cleveland. It was displayed there from 2002-2004

The Beatles Looking Back: The Final Trip

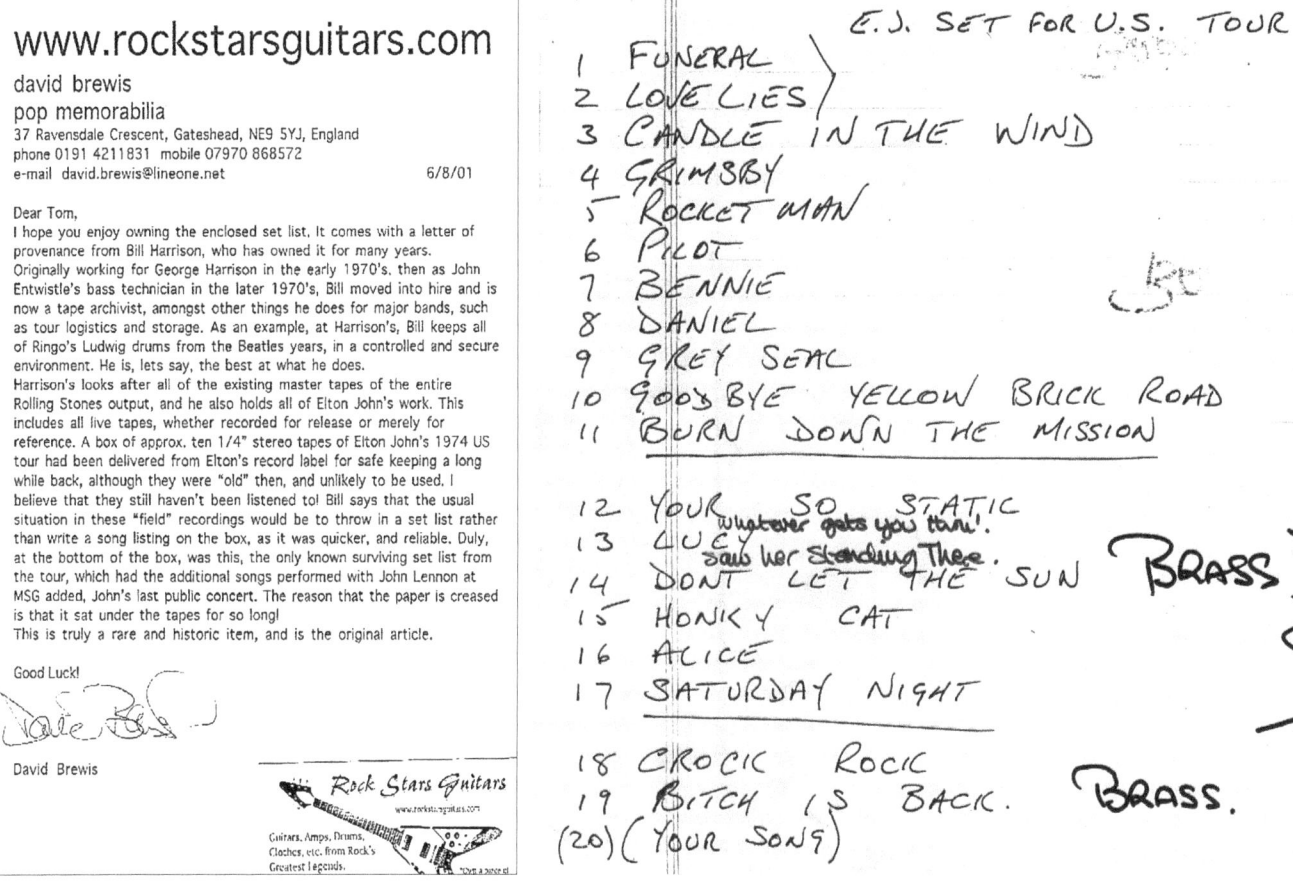

The letter from David Brewis, at left, accompanied the set list from that night (on right) when I bought it. Note the added songs for John Lennon's encore appearance.

"What I have to say is all in the music.
If I want to say anything, I write a song."
— Paul McCartney

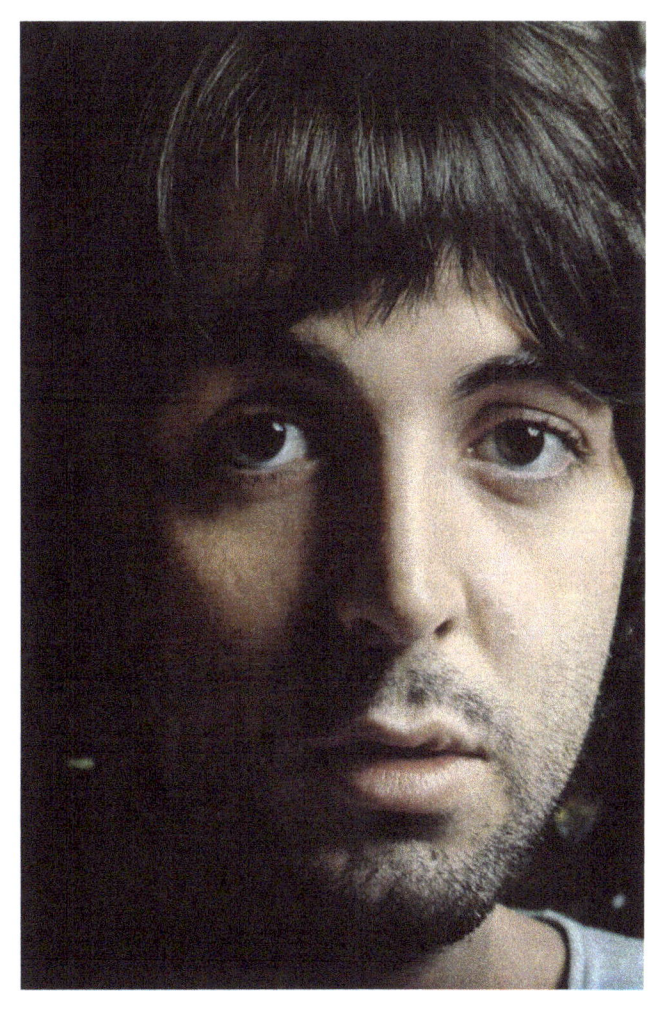

Paul McCartney

"It's like you're an astronaut and you've been to the moon, what do you want to do with the rest of your life?"
— Paul McCartney

The Beatles Looking Back: The Final Trip

The handwritten note at right was signed by Paul to a fan on the back of a Beatles Parlophone card (above) in early 1963.

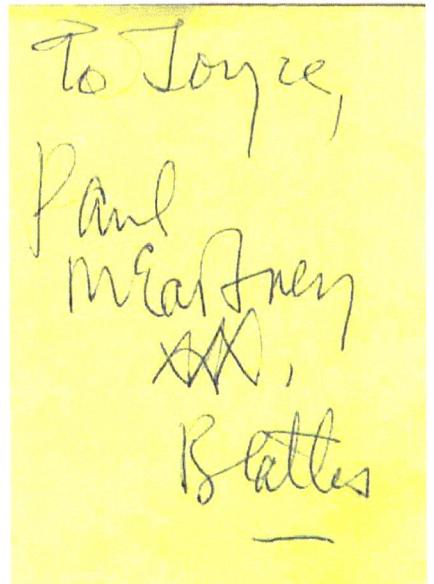

A very nice early example of Paul McCartney's autograph with inscription from late 1961 to early 1962, left.

Paul McCartney signed pages from an autograph book during Beatlemania, above.

The Beatles Looking Back: The Final Trip

> I the undersigned believe this item to be absolutely genuine.
> I started a second hand shop called "Guzunders" in 1977 in the center of my home town, Bournemouth. After a very short time it developed into a vintage clothing shop. I had to move to larger premises and called the new shop "Bizarre Bazaar". I found myself catering for clothing dealers from all over the world and film and tv companys.
> In the early 1980s a local gentleman turned up at the shop and sold me a large quantity of mens clothing. He explained that these items had been left with him for various reasons. Mostly the items came from Dean Martin who had lived here in the UK for approx two years. Most of these items had Mr Martins name embroidered on the insides. I sold most of them from my shop and the better items I sold through "Christies" south Kensington, London.
> The gentleman explained that he had also driven Mr Paul McCartney whilst he was appearing at a theatre here in Bournemouth with the Beatles and that the jacket had also been left with him. He had held on to these items for approx. 20 years and had decided to sell them as he was moving to a smaller house and no longer had the room to hold on to them. With the jacket also came the autograph which he said had been signed for a then teenaged member of his family. I have kept the jacket for approx. 20 years.
> I have no reason to disbelieve the gentleman as there seemed no reason why he was not telling the truth. I paid cash for all the items which he bought to my shop in his car. Unfortunatley I did not take his name.
> Thankyou.
>
> James Hardy.

Paul McCartney's dark blue, collarless performance jacket from 1963, accompanied by an autograph page signed by McCartney to his chauffeur's daughter, Estelle. Paul left the jacket in the car and the chauffeur kept it.

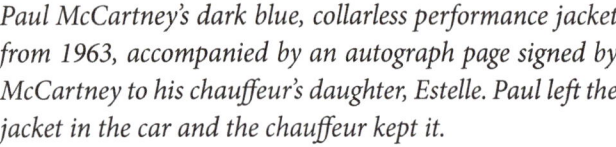

Paul signed a 1965 US Tour book page featuring his picture and added a little humor.

The Beatles Looking Back: The Final Trip

Paul's autograph: from S.F. Hilton in 1964 when Beatles played Cow Palace.

A friend, Dovie, was able to get Paul's autograph as she worked @ the Hilton in Housekeeping.

These liquor sets were put in all "VIP" rooms for their enjoyment!

Narissa di Lucia

the enclosed autograph dates from 64/65, acquired when my mother was working in Broadgreen Hospital, Liverpool. Paul came in to visit Rory Storm.

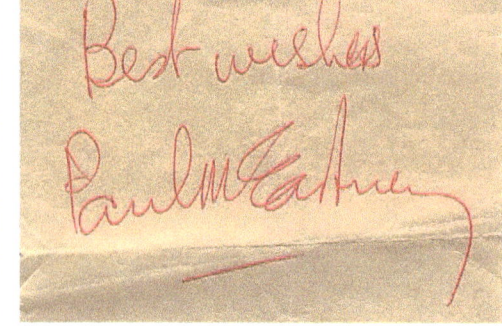

Left is a Paul McCartney signed calendar page from The Beatle years in 1966.

The Beatles Looking Back: The Final Trip

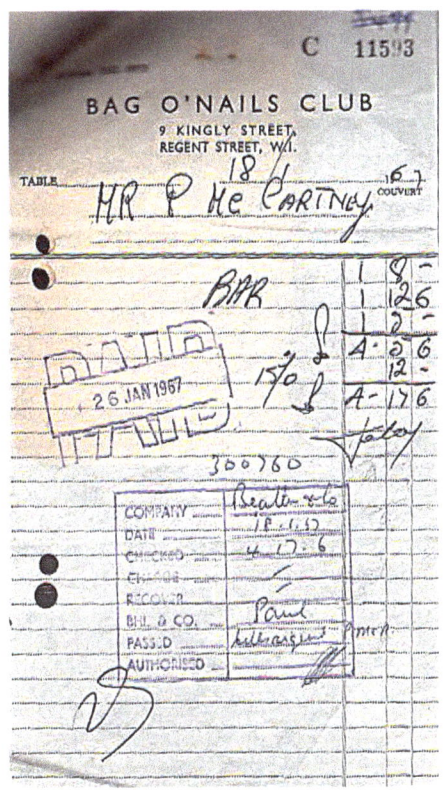
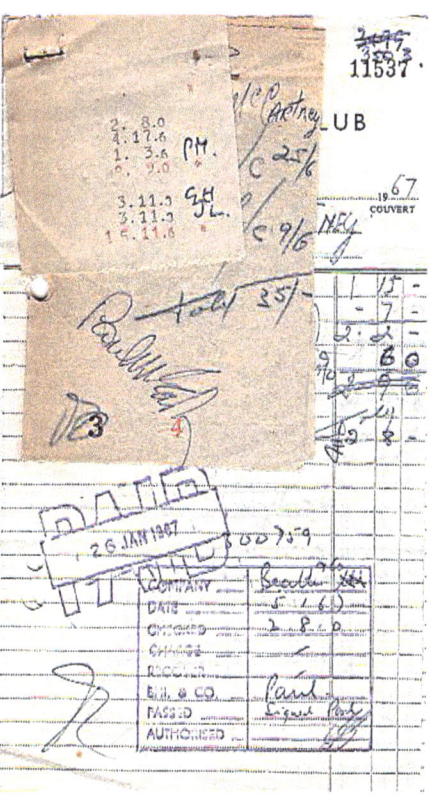
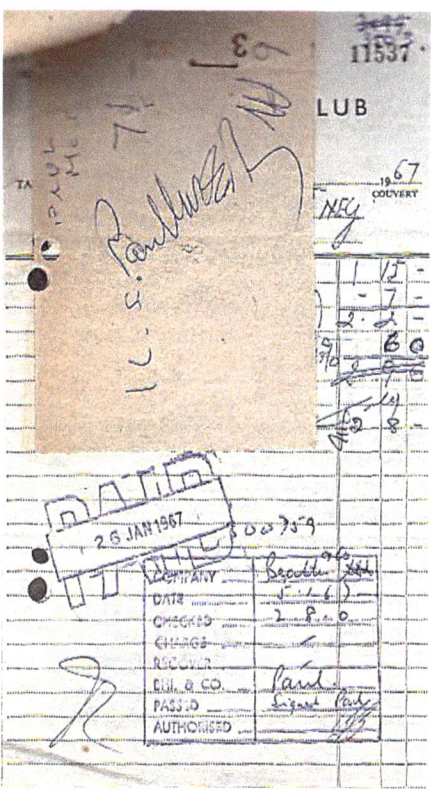
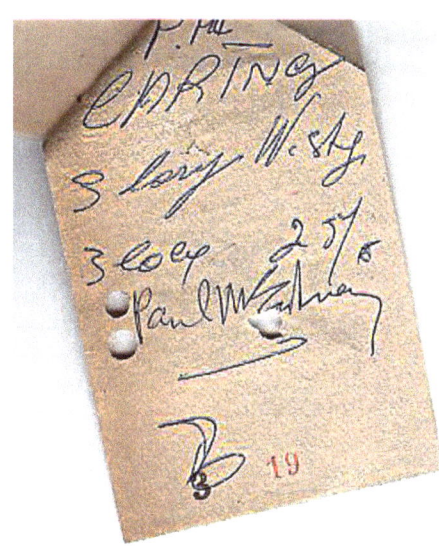

An extremely rare set of receipts from the Bag O' Nails music nightclub in London, 1967. Paul has signed the receipts. This is the club where Paul met his first wife, Linda.

This is Paul's international vaccination form from 1968. It was required for the trip he and John Lennon made to New York to announce Apple Records in May 1968.

McCartney Productions contract from 1970, the year The Beatles disbanded, signed by Paul McCartney (Director) and his wife, Linda McCartney.

The Beatles Looking Back: The Final Trip

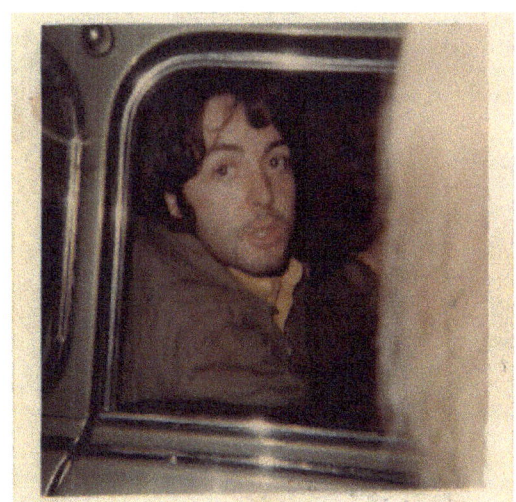

An incredible assortment of one-of-a-kind candid snap shots of Paul McCartney, all signed in the late 1960s when McCartney was still with The Beatles. Very rare!

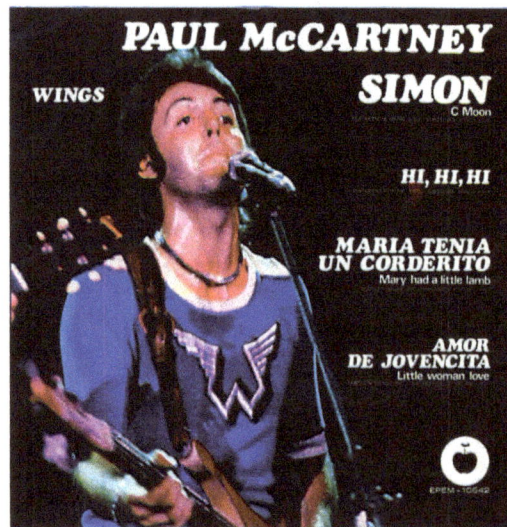

Paul McCartney did not rest on his laurels after the The Beatles broke up in April of 1970. In 1971, he formed the group Wings, which included his wife, Linda, and former Moody Blues guitarist and singer Denny Laine. Wings played several small clubs and schools, and they sometimes just showed up in their tour bus unannounced. Early Wings items are scarce, but anything regarding the stage is almost unheard of.

Above is Paul McCartney's stage-worn Wings shirt from 1971. There are many photos of Paul wearing the shirt during this concert tour in 1971. Paul donated this shirt to a charity in the early 1970s. Several years ago, in a private conversation, Paul was shown a picture of the shirt and he recalled it and confirmed that he gave it to a charity in the '70s.

BAND ON THE RUN

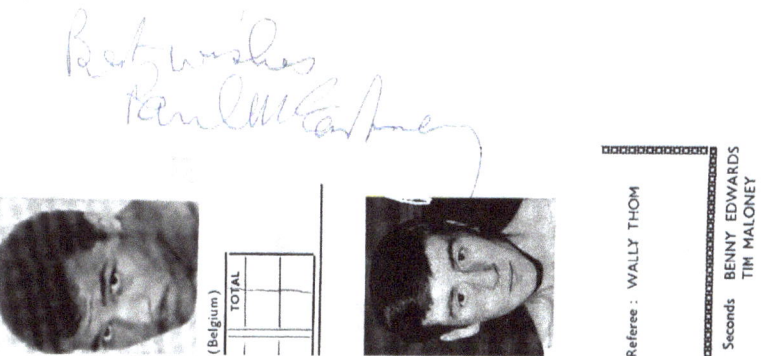

Paul McCartney attended a boxing match on March 13, 1973 to see John Conteh fight, but also to invite him, along with other celebrities, to be in the photo shoot for the Band on the Run cover. The program was signed by Paul that night and reads: "Best Wishes Paul McCartney". John Conteh also agreed to be on the cover of the album.

This Band on the Run album cover is signed on the back with lengthy inscriptions by Paul and Linda McCartney to director John Landis. I learned about this particular piece when I was in a Hollywood shop and started talking about autographs with the owner. He told me about this album and shared his story of how he got it from John Landis. After that, I just had to have it! It is one of the nicest signed Band on the Run covers I've ever seen. This was a true find!

Venus and Mars are alright tonight.

Denny Laine, former Moody Blues member in the 1960s, joined Paul and Linda when they formed Wings in the early 1970s. This is an incredibly rare handwritten lyric for the song "No Words", written by Denny, was included on the Band on the Run album which was released in 1973. Denny wrote the lyric on the back of a Venus and Mars promo card. He also signed the front.

Band on the Run *album cover signed on the back by Paul McCartney.*

A Paul McCartney and Wings color 8x10, signed by Paul, Linda, Denny Laine, Jimmy McCulloch, and Joe English in 1976.

A fold out poster from the Venus and Mars album, signed by Paul, Linda, Denny Laine and Jimmy McCulloch, with Paul's signature and inscription enlarged above.

WINGS 1976

This Wings Fan Club folder card was signed in the centerfold in 1976 by Paul McCartney, Linda McCartney and Denny Laine.

The Beatles Looking Back: The Final Trip

This Linda's Pix for Seventy Six *picture book and calendar, is signed on an inside page both Paul and Linda McCartney.*

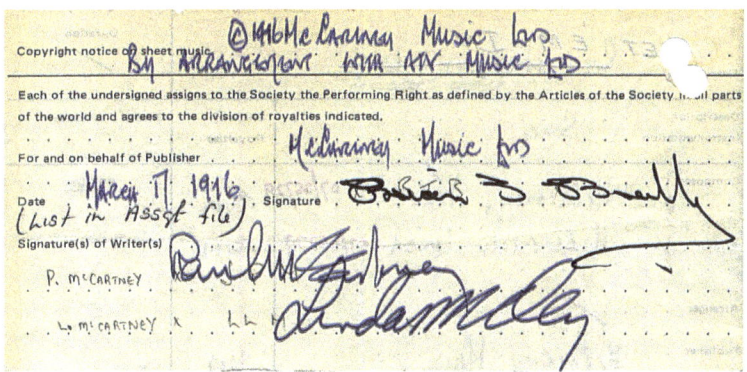 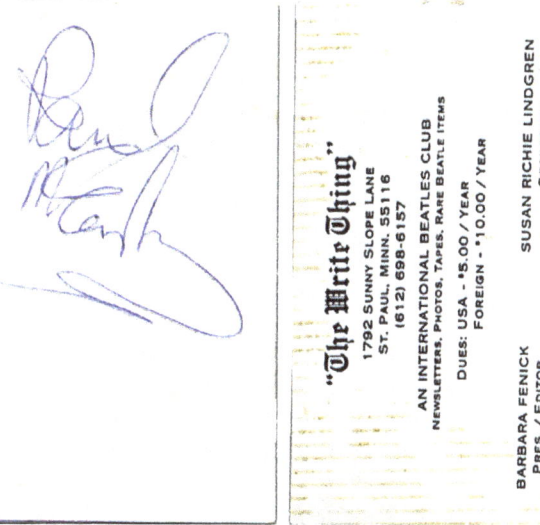

This is a copyright notice rider for 1976 McCartney Music, signed by Paul and Linda on the back (shown above).

Barb Fenick, president/editor of The Write Thing International Beatles Club, was met Paul and asked him to sign the back of her business card.

The Beatles Looking Back: The Final Trip

This Daily Mirror British Poll Awards final results flyer, left, includes Wings winning Best Rock and Pop Group. It was signed nicely by Paul and Linda McCartney in 1976.

This Strat Squire Guitar, right, was signed on the body by Paul McCartney in the late 1980s. It is pretty rare to obtain the signature on the body as most are signed on the pic guard making this quite scarce.

This 1979 group Wings fan club card, left, was signed by the whole group: Paul McCartney, Linda McCartney, Denny Laine, Lawrence Juber, and Steve Holly.

The Beatles Looking Back: The Final Trip

WINGS 1979

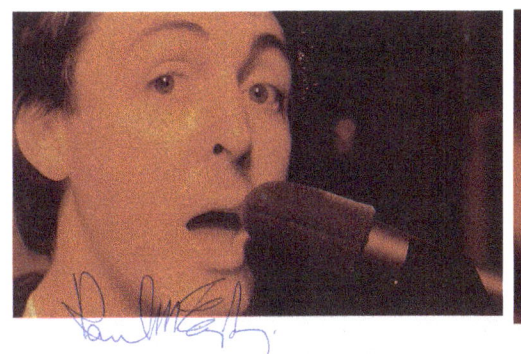

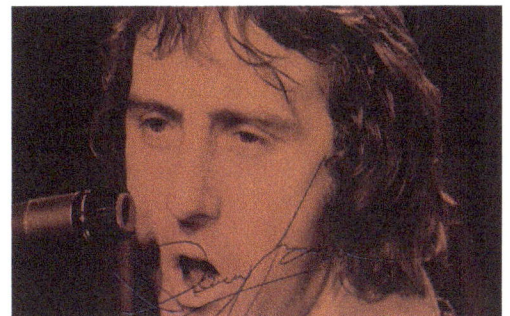

A set of individually signed 1979 Wings Fan Club Cards.

The Beatles Looking Back: The Final Trip

PAUL McCARTNEY Photo by Linda McCartney

Promotional 8x10 photo taken by Linda McCartney for of Paul's release of McCartney 2 signed by Paul, adding "all the best" from 1980.

A nice signature of Paul McCartney on an autograph book page from 2/20/1980.

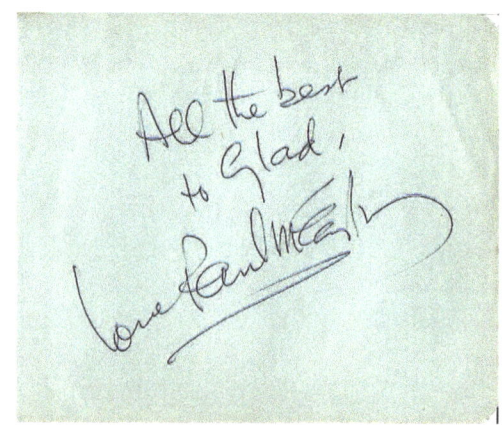

Autograph album page signed and inscribed by Paul from the 1980s.

A Hard Days Night *movie poster for the re-release in 1982, signed on the bottom right hand corner by Paul McCartney.*

A bank money envelope with the words "Merry Christmas" and added mistletoe, signed by Paul McCartney. This became an extra gift for the recipient as well. Happy Krimble as Paul would say during the holiday season during the days of Beatle-mania.

This menu from The Four Seasons was signed and inscribed by Paul McCartney, obtained in the 1980s.

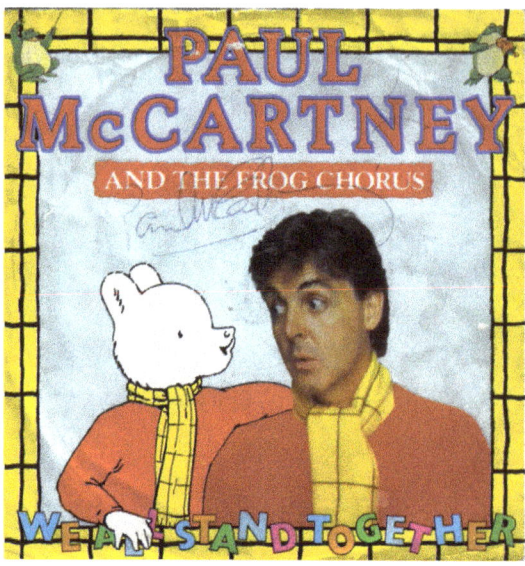

Paul has signed a 1984 contest questionnaire used to promote his movie, Give My Regards to Broadstreet, writing: "Congratulations you winner you! All the best Paul McCartney".

We All Stand Together, an album featuring *Paul McCartney and the Frog Chorus*, was made for the animated short film *Rupert* and the Frog Song *that came out in 1984. The album was written and produced by Paul McCartney. The Rupert character was taken based on a comic strip that first appeared in the* Daily Express *in November of 1920. Paul has signed the picture sleeve at the top, just under the title.*

The Beatles Looking Back: The Final Trip

This Beatles 1967-1970 album cover signed was the centerfold: "All the best Paul McCartney". It was signed in the early 1980s.

This Strat Squire guitar was signed nicely on the pic guard by Paul. The signature is from the late 1980s or early 1990s.

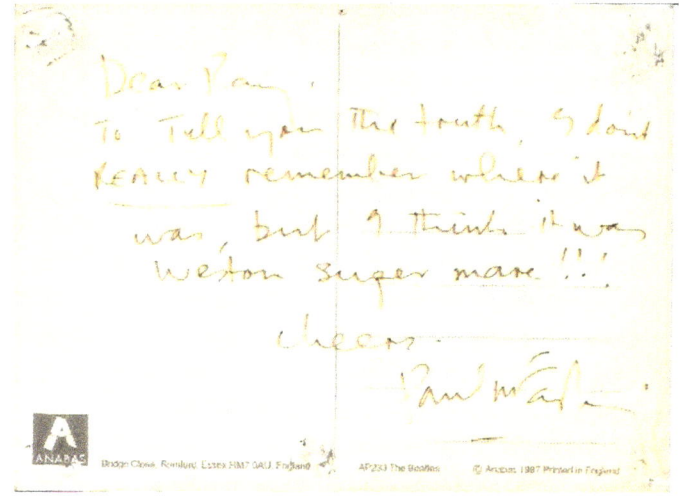

An original 1960s Beatles postcard with a handwritten note recalling the location where the photo was taken.

The Beatles Looking Back: The Final Trip

This original 1963 Cavern membership card from Liverpool is signed on the front by Paul Mccartney.

This matted candid photograph was taken of Paul McCartney on stage during his Wings Over America Tour. It is signed on the photograph and matting by Paul.

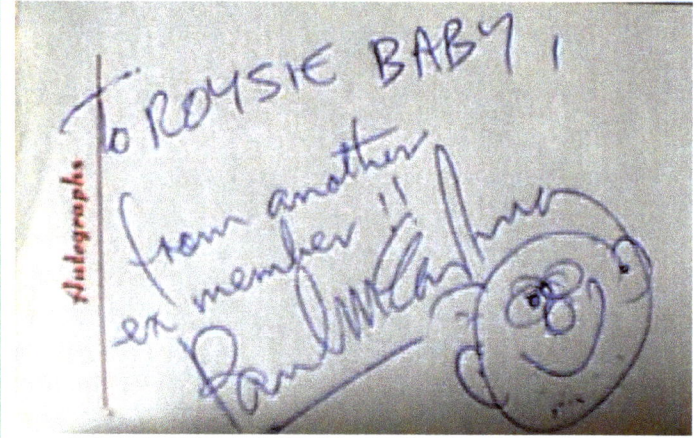

This original 1964 Cavern membership card from Liverpool is signed on the inside page with the inscription: "from another ex member" and Paul has also drawn a smiley face below his signature.

A unique color photo of Paul McCartney made up like a clown has been nicely signed by Paul, with an inscription and added smiley face.

The Beatles Looking Back: The Final Trip

Thank You Very Much, Mike McCartney's Family Album *is signed and inscribed by Paul, who added a smiley face on the testimonial page. His brother also inscribed it and signed it "Mike Mac"..*

The Beatles Looking Back: The Final Trip

Above, a holiday greeting card to a family friend in Paul McCartney's handwriting. He also added a face doodle.

At right, another holiday greeting card signed by Paul McCartney (who also signed for Linda).

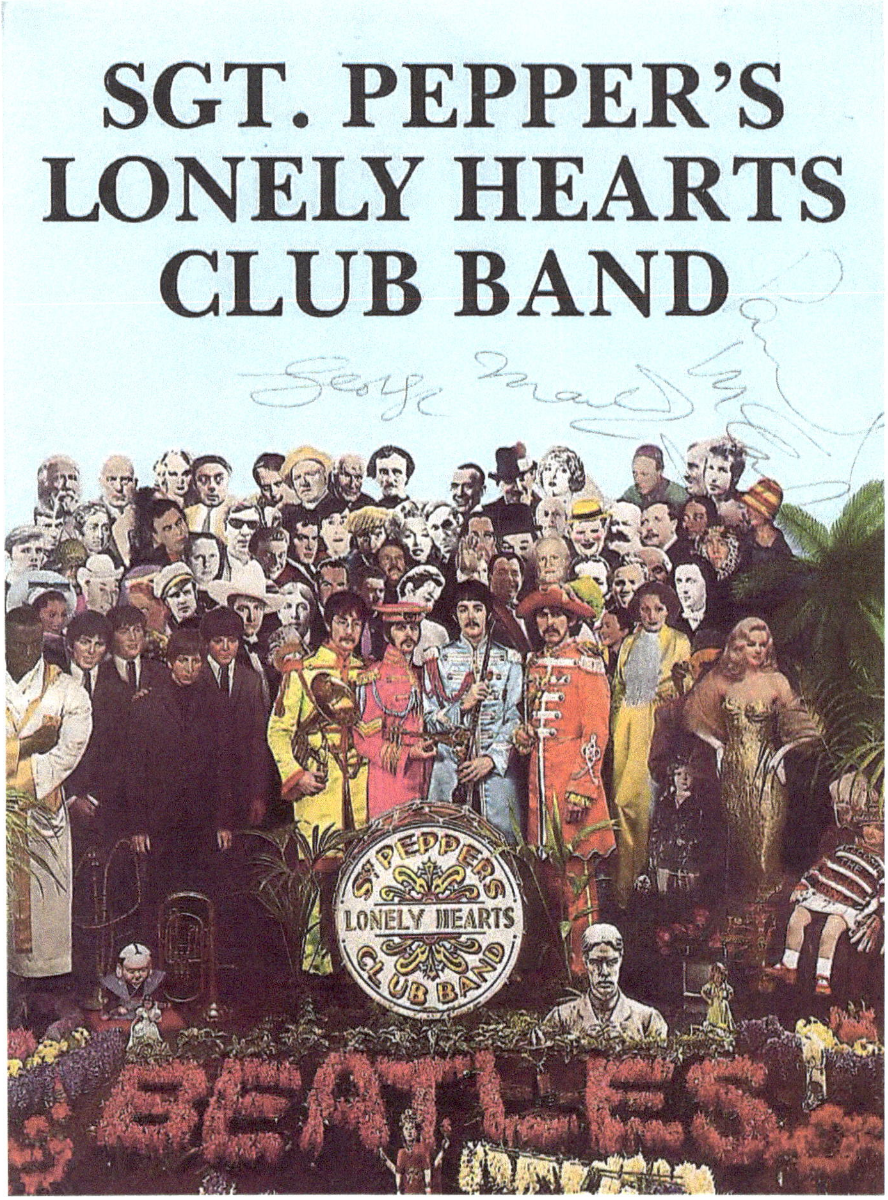

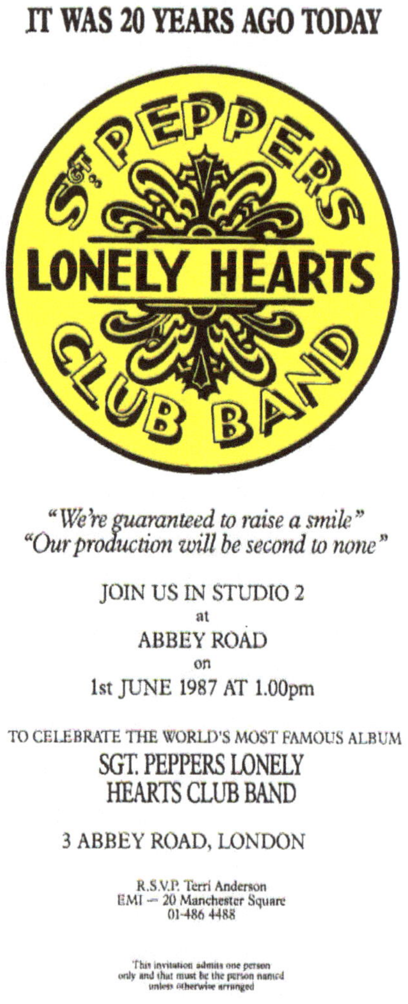

IT WAS 20 YEARS AGO TODAY

SGT. PEPPERS LONELY HEARTS CLUB BAND

"We're guaranteed to raise a smile"
"Our production will be second to none"

JOIN US IN STUDIO 2
at
ABBEY ROAD
on
1st JUNE 1987 AT 1.00pm

TO CELEBRATE THE WORLD'S MOST FAMOUS ALBUM
SGT. PEPPERS LONELY
HEARTS CLUB BAND

3 ABBEY ROAD, LONDON

R.S.V.P. Terri Anderson
EMI — 20 Manchester Square
01-486 4488

This invitation admits one person
only and that must be the person named
unless otherwise arranged

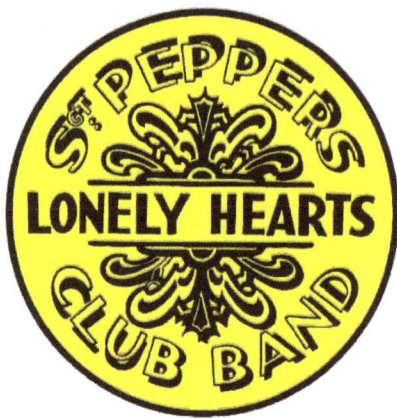

An RSVP event celebrating the 20th anniverasry of the release of the Sgt. Pepper album took place at Abbey Road Studios on June 1, 1987. The original invitation ticket and the press kit, pictured above, are signed on the front by attendees Paul McCartney and Beatles record producer George Martin. This is the only signed item I am aware of from that event, as it was a invitation-only gathering

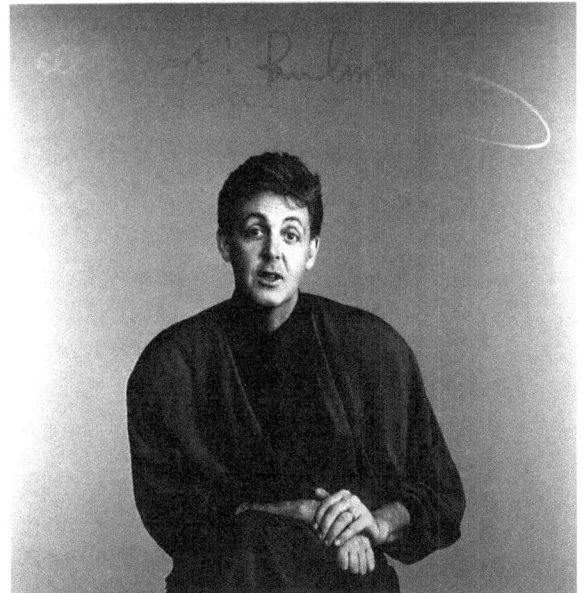

Paul McCartney's All the Best *box set collection, containing 7" records but also two photos — one with a preprinted autograph at the top (shown left) and another of the same pose that was signed by Paul in 1987 (the same year the boxed set was released). He wrote: "To Amanda, Cheers" and added his signature.*

Very seldom do you get the opportunity to own something given to a friend or family member of an artist, but I was fortunate enough to obtain this incredible pick guard signed by Paul McCartney, along with the envelope the guard was housed in. Paul dedicated the envelope and added a smiley face. Later the pick guard was applied on a Hoefner Bass.

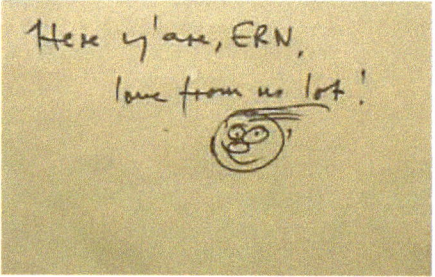

 A few years after that, I was lucky enough to obtain another pick guard, shown at left, that was signed by Paul for a family member and also applied to a Hoefner. It was great to have the opportunity to have both of these historical items in my collection.

The Beatles Looking Back: The Final Trip

This promotional postcard from 1989 is signed by Paul McCartney. This was likely done around the time of the release of the *Flowers in the Dirt* album.

This inner yellow sleeve from the album *Flowers in the Dirt* has been signed by Paul McCartney, Linda McCartney, Wix Wickens, Hamish Stuart, Robbie McIntosh, and Chris Whitten.

This Paul McCartney 1989–1990 US Tour book, right, is signed by Paul and includes pictures from the day of the signing.

This Paul McCartney free handout booklet for 1989–1990 concert tour is signed on the front cover by Paul. The book and signature were obtained during the tour. What makes this special for me is that I purchased this from one of Paul's mates from his Liverpool days, Sam Leach.

A second Paul McCartney free handout booklet signed nicely on the front cover by Paul.

Paul McCartney and his new band first announced their upcoming tour on November 22, 1989 at the Lyceum Theatre in New York City during well-organized press conference. Once the group left, a quick-thinking fan grabbed the cup Paul had drinking from, then I purchased it from him. I thought it was cool because the press conference was recorded and when I watched the film, I could see Paul using the mug. When I purchased it, the mug had not been washed and still had Paul's fingerprints on it.

The Beatles Looking Back: The Final Trip

I certify that this book with the autographs was signed by Paul, Linda plus the band Backstage at Philadelphia 1990.

Tony Scott

13 METHUEN ST
L'POOL 15
ENGLAND
U.K.

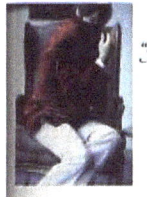

"I'm not trying to impress anyone except myself."

Paul McCartney

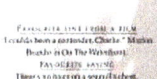

This Paul McCartney Let It be Liverpool concert ticket from June 28, 1990 is signed: "all the best Paul McCartney" and was obtained in person after that show

Paul McCartney's Flowers In The Dirt cassette cover signed on the front by Paul and inside by Linda McCartney in 1989

Paul McCartney's promotional card for the song "Birthday" from his upcoming live album, Tripping the Live Fantastic. It was signed and inscribed by Paul in 1990.

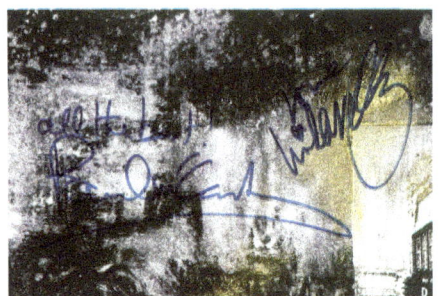

This poster from the 1989 Flowers in the Dirt *World Tour Pack is signed by Paul McCartney, Linda McCartney, Wix Wickens, Hamish Stuart, Robbie McIntosh, and Chris Whitten.*

The Beatles Looking Back: The Final Trip

Two promotional posters advertising Paul McCartney's album Flowers in the Dirt, *and another for the America tour were signed by Paul in 1989.*

An autographed program from Paul McCartney's Liverpool Oratorio *in 1991.*

This hand-drawn pencil sketch of flowers in a vase was dedicated and signed by Paul and Linda McCartney. The date at the top reads 16/1/90.

The Beatles Looking Back: The Final Trip

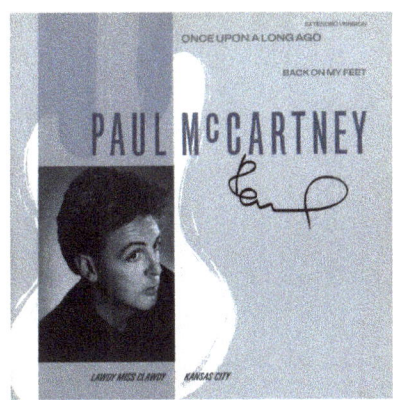

This Paul McCartney 12" single "Once Upon a Long Ago" is signed on the front with his sir name. Paul released this in 1987.

Paul McCartney's album Tug of War, released in 1982, *was signed on the front with an inscription by Paul McCartney.*

This copy of McCartney's album, Unplugged, released in 1991, was signed and dedicated by Paul on the front cover.

This 1991 Paul McCartney fan club magazine, Club Sandwich, *was signed signed on the front by Paul, Linda, Mitch Mitchell (of the Jimi Hendrix Experience), and Beatles movies co-star Victor Spinetti.*

The Beatles Looking Back: The Final Trip

Paul McCartney's Run Devil Run CD cover was signed on the front in 1999.

This 1993 New World Tour program was signed on the front by Paul. This was given to fans who purchased the LIPA package, which included the sound check and the concert.

Paul McCartney's generic white label promo "Hope of Deliverance" from the Off the Ground album generic white cover signed nicely by Paul with inscription from 1993

Paul McCartney's 1997 Flaming Pie CD cover signed on the front with "all the best".

Linda McCartney's compilation CD, Wide Prairie, *compiled by Paul, was released posthumously in October 1998, just six months after Linda's passing. Paul has signed on his image on the inside front cover and placed a heart on Linda's photo. There are very few signed copies of this CD.*

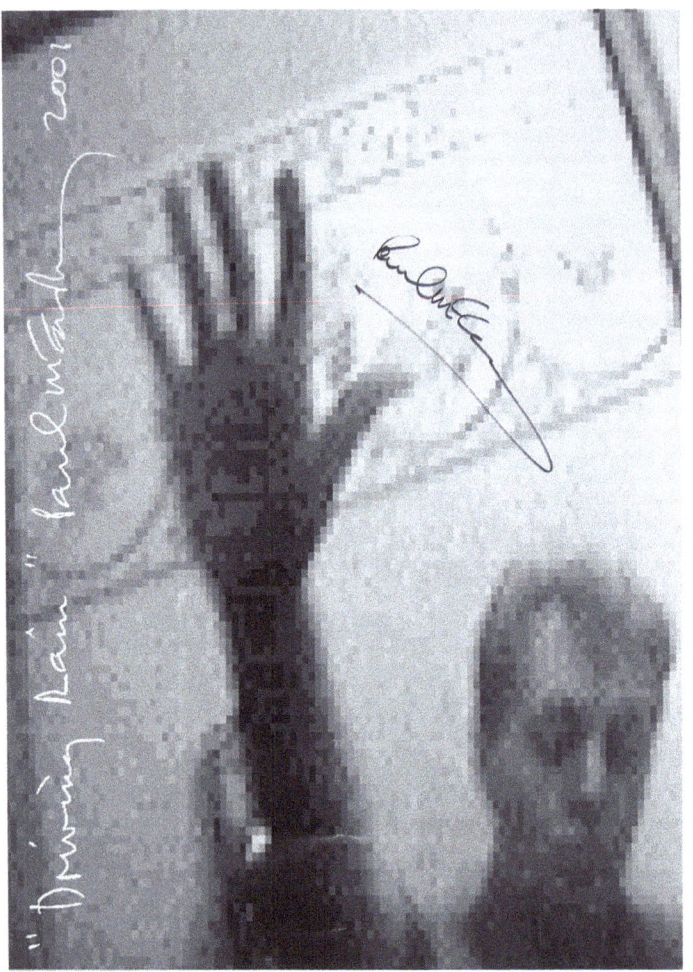

A signed promotional poster for the album Driving Rain, released in 2001.

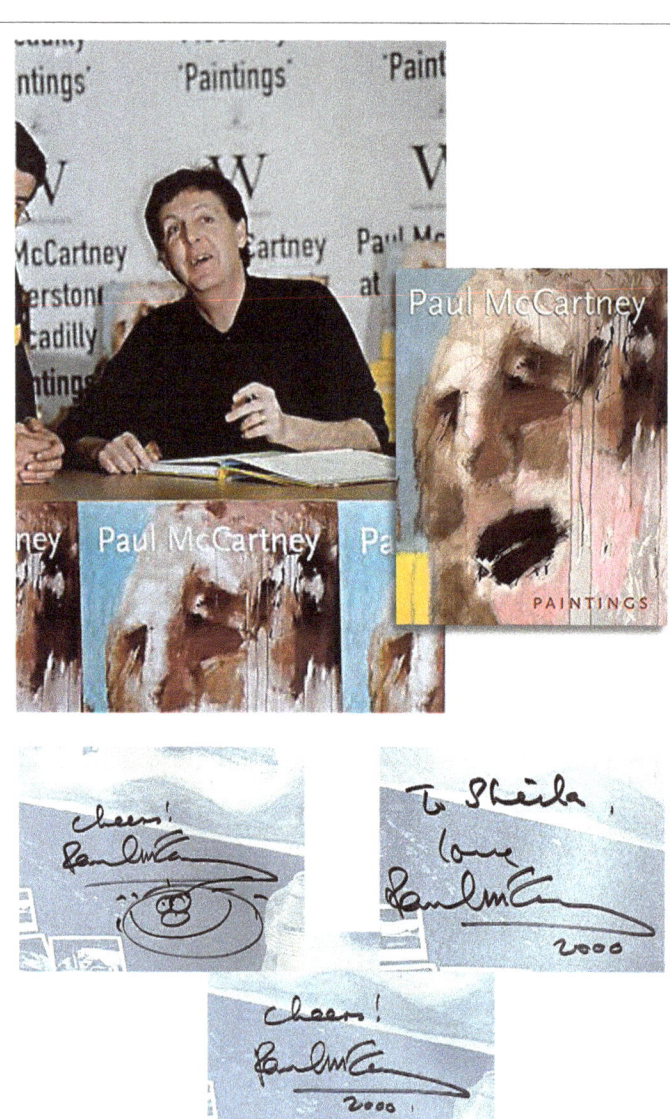

Paul McCartney met his fans at a book signing for Paintings in 2000. I was fortunate to be able to purchase several copies. I've included some samples.

The Beatles Looking Back: The Final Trip

I was able to pick up a few signed copies of Paul McCartney's book, Blackbird Singing, from people who obtained them at a book signing he did in 2001. I have included some samples.

PAUL SIGNS FOR HIS FANS
IN LIVERPOOL AND THE WORLD THROUGH THE YEARS

The Beatles Looking Back: The Final Trip

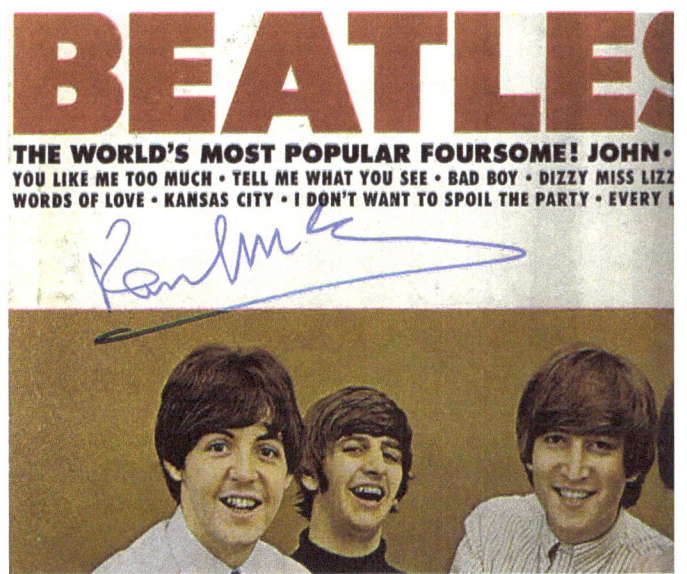

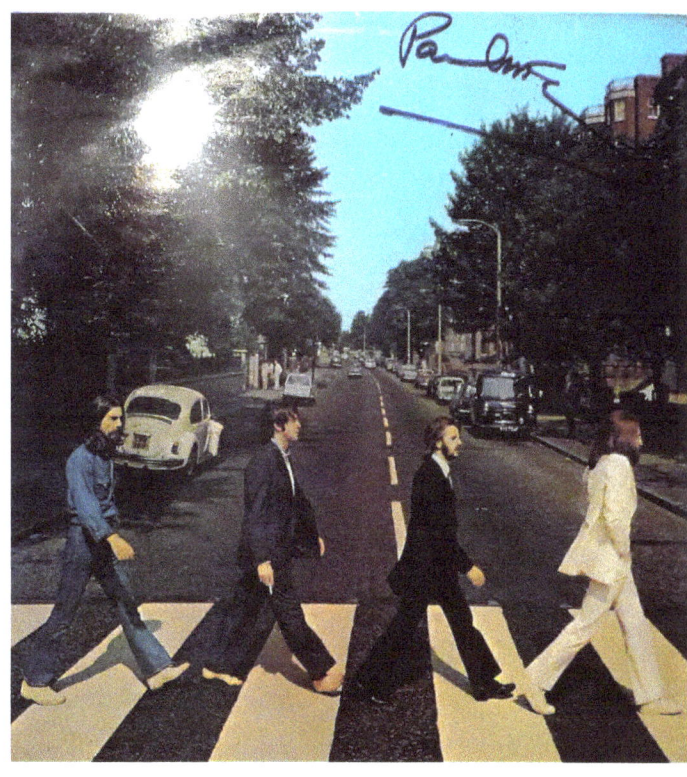

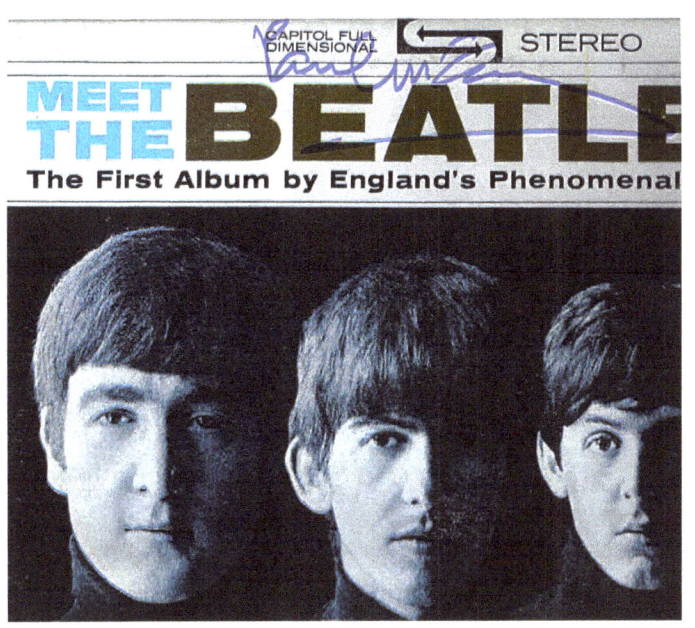

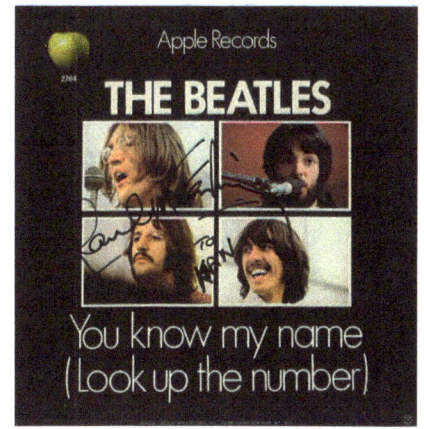

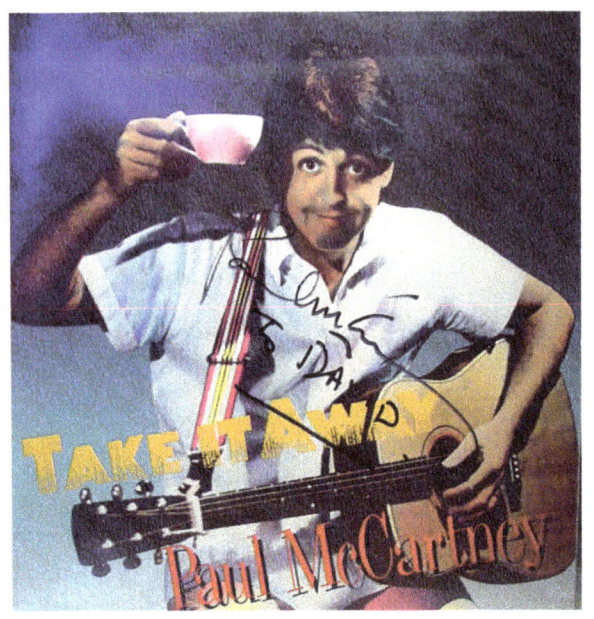

The Fireman *album cover was autographed:* "Cheers John" *by Paul McCartney. This signature was obtained at a signing event promoting the album release in London. I purchased the signed album directly from John.*

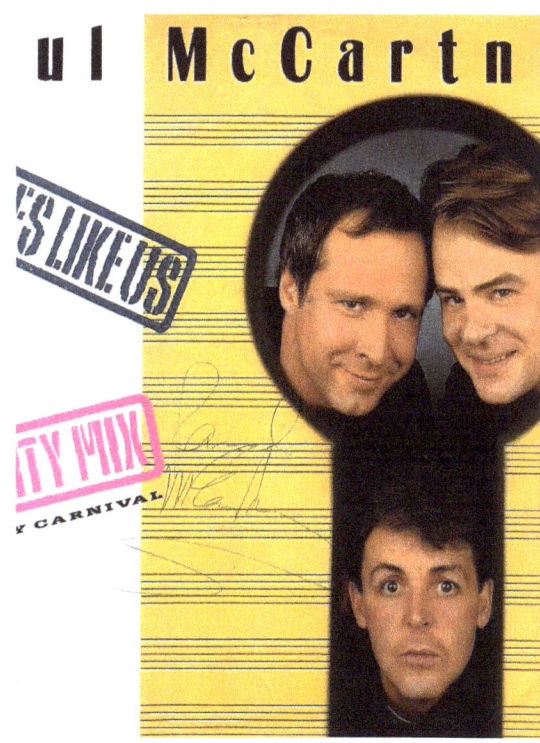

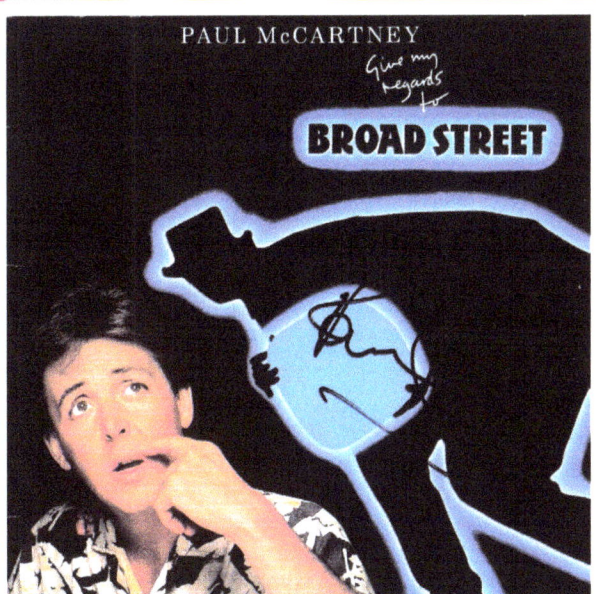

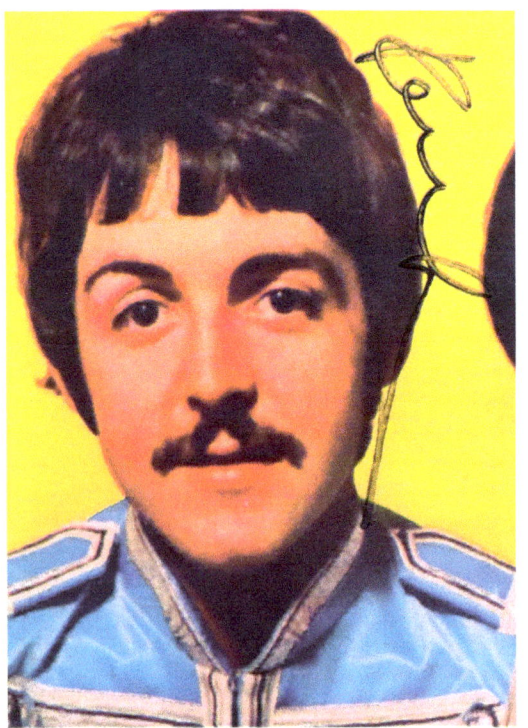

> Tom,
>
> Paul McCartney signed this album in Seattle while on Tour in 2002. He signed it before the show at his hotel, The Four Seasons, now known as The Olympic. When he was leaving the hotel his security lined everyone up as Paul skipped to his limo, he then rolled down the window and we got to go to the window one at a time to receive an autograph. In 2002 his signature was at it's weakest, typically signing just "Paul" with an underline as in this case. I late had this album certified by PSA/DNA.
>
> Regards,
> Justin Maser   6-18-2009

The Beatles Looking Back: The Final Trip

The Beatles Looking Back: The Final Trip

The Beatles Looking Back: The Final Trip

The star-studded benefit for Hole in the Wall Camps, founded by Paul Newman in 1988, took place on April 21, 2005, at Lincoln Center's Avery Fisher Hall in New York. Paul Newman, Paul McCartney, Julia Roberts, Robin Williams, Tony Bennett, and many others were in attendance. This Stars in the Sky benefit program has been signed on the front by Paul McCartney, Paul Newman, Tony Bennett, and Robin Williams. The Association of Hole in the Wall Camps now includes nine camps and served over 10,000 children in 2005.

Paul McCartney attended The Queen's Jubilee in Mayfair, London on May 23, 2012. After the event, a lucky fan obtained Paul's autograph on this Russian Balalaika guitar. Also included with the guitar is a photo of Paul just after he signed it. He is pictured with the fan in the background holding the signed guitar. A detailed letter also accompanied the guitar. The Russian instrument relates to words Paul penned in 1968 to the song "Back in the USSR". In my experience, this is the only known signed Balalaika.

Beatlefest

Among the events and activities at Beatlefest are
nightly concerts by Beatles tribute band Liverpool,
appearances and performances by various musical guests,
photo exhibits, panels and discussions with authors and Beatles experts,
movie screenings, live auctions, a Beatles sound-alike contest,
a Beatles marketplace, and more.

BEATLESFEST ... MY MEMORIES

I attended my first Beatles Fest Convention in 1982. Remember, this was before the days of the internet and social media, so the only way you could celebrate The Beatles with friends old and new was to attend one of these conventions each year. My first was in Chicago.

I loved the anticipation of looking forward to the event each year, knowing everything there would be about my favorite group. It was always such a good time. My wife, Mary, and I attended all the Chicago Beatlesfests from 1982 through 2010.

One of the bonuses to attending was developing friendships with fellow fans. The rest of the events, including seeing the special guests and experiencing the massive Beatles Flea Market filled with memorabilia, some of wich was for sale, icing on the cake for me was was atttending the Beatles auction each year. You just never knew what collectible Beatles gems would be there to bid on.

We were fortunate enough to atend the 1989 Los Angeles Beatlefest. Paul McCartney was in town then to play at the fabulous Los Angeles Forum, which created an extra buzz the entire weekend.

We also attended the Beatlesfest in New Jersey where we met fellow fans I'd only spoken to on the phone prior to that. The real highlight for us was meeting the Walter Shenson, Beatles movie producer, who invited us to be in a documentary about the movie *A Hard Day's Night*. The documentary was hosted by Phil Collins, and yes, we made it into the final cut of the documentary. Walter was a true gentleman and we

enjoyed our conversation with him immensely. (Sadly, he passed away on October 17, 2000.)

Because my collection had become so well know, in 2005 I was honored to be associated with The Beatle Brunch team featuring Joe Johnson who does the weekly broadcast celebrating the music and lives of the Fab Four.

Johnson often featured me in his broadcasts and would post stories about my collection on his website. To promote the Beatle Brunch, Joe and the Beatles Brunch family would attend the fest, ant they were kind enough to invite me to the party to set up items from my Beatles collection.

Those were times hold a special place in my heart. I loved to interact with other fans and colletors who enjoyed The Beatles. It was a special thrill that they enjoyed viewing my collection so much too

It has been years since I attended a Beatlesfest, but I will never forget the fond memories these conventions provided for me or the group that inspired them.

Tom Fontaine

FRIENDS AT THE FEST

Downstairs at The Marketplace, from left to right, Marty Eck, Jim Cunningham, Mike Hollander, Jay Benjamin and, yes, that's me!

Wayne Rogers and my wife, Mary.

THE FEATURED GUESTS

Mary with Paul's guitarist and former Pretender, Robbie McIntosh in 2000.

Paul's bass player and former member of The Average-White Band, Hamish Stuart, right, at the flea Market in 2001.

The Beatles Looking Back: The Final Trip

Mary with John Lennon's original group, The Quarrymen, in 2007.

Mary with singer Donavon in 2003.

Mary with Denny Laine, Wings guitarist, in 2005.

Sid Bernstein, The Beatles Shea Stadium promoter, in 2001

Mary with George Harrison's former wife, Patti Boyd, in 2008.

Victor Spinetti, who appeared in all three movies with The Beatles, in 2007.

Klauss Voormann, photographer and friend to The Beatles in the early days in Germany, in 2001.

The Beatles Looking Back: The Final Trip

Ronnie Spector, former Ronnette, with Mary in 2009.

Joe Johnson, Beatle Bruch radio host, with Mary in 2008.

Mark Hudson, from the Hudson Brothers, with Mary in 2003

Lizzie Bravo, original Apple Scruff Girl, in 2003.

Downstairs at the Marketplace in 2002.

My Beatles display at The Beatle Brunch table in August 2006.

My Beatles display at the Beatle Brunch table in August 2008.

My Beatles display at The Beatle Brunch table in August 2010.

George Harrison

"The Beatles saved the world from boredom."
— George Harrison

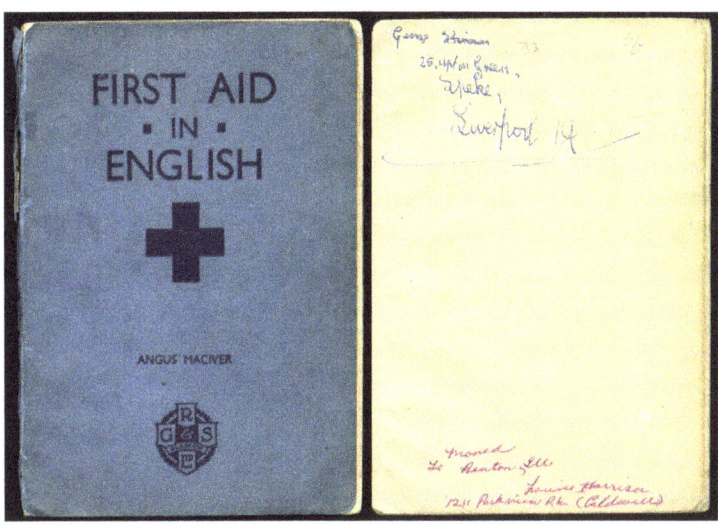

George Harrison's personally owned first aid book, used at the Liverpool grammar school he attended.

George's signature on a small autograph book page from 1962.

The Beatles 1964 US tour book dedicated to Jill and signed by George Harrison.

The Beatles Looking Back: The Final Trip

A Beatles promotional card with a nice handwritten note from George Harrison to a fan on the back. He also mentions their latest release "She Loves You" from 1963.

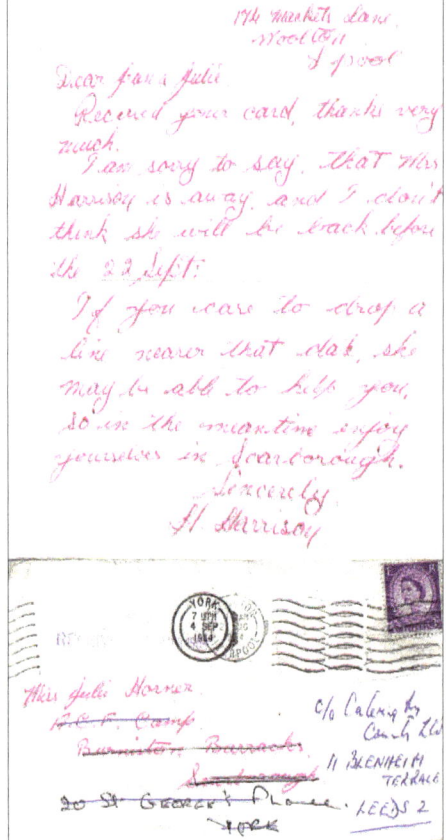

Often George's parents would get fan mail intended for him, and were gracious enough to respond for him. Here are two letters from George's mother and father to his fans.

A very nice Christmas card from George and Patti Harrison to actress Haley Mills and family, (including actor John Mills). This one's quite rare!

A Beatles Monthly *book from 1966, signed in the centerfold by George on his image.*

The Beatles Looking Back: The Final Trip

When an unplanned opportunity arises to meet a Beatle or any celebrity, you have to find something for them to autograph for you to commemorate the occasion. This is exactly what happened in the 1960s with the recipient of this signature. George was asked to sign on the front of a candid photo of the recipient, seen at right.

A handwritten note signed nicely by George on dark purple stationery which is how the letter was represented in 1966.

In-person signatures on different pieces of paper by George, who wrote: "To Janice, love George Harrison" as well as a signature from Patti Harrison. These were both obtained in the 1960s.

George Harrison's suit manufactured by Lord John of Carnaby St., as indicated by the label found inside the suite. This two-piece tweed suit from circa 1968 was made in Italy, and both owned and worn by George. He donated it to Madame Tussaud's Wax Museum in London, and the black and white photo on the right shows the suite on a wax figure at Madame Tussaud's in the late 1960s.

The Beatles Looking Back: The Final Trip

George Harrison's signed checks from 1970 and 1971.

A nice signature from George Harrison
clipped from a document

The Beatles Looking Back: The Final Trip

George Harrison's signature on a promotional photo from 1970.

The Beatles Looking Back: The Final Trip

This 1974 tour book from George's US tour with Ravi Shankar and Billy Preston, is signed and dedicated on the inside by George, who also has drawn the Sanskrit symbol OM (or AUM), the symbol of the essence of Hinduism

This menu for a flight from Los Angeles to London is dedicated to lucky fans and was signed on August 10, 1975.

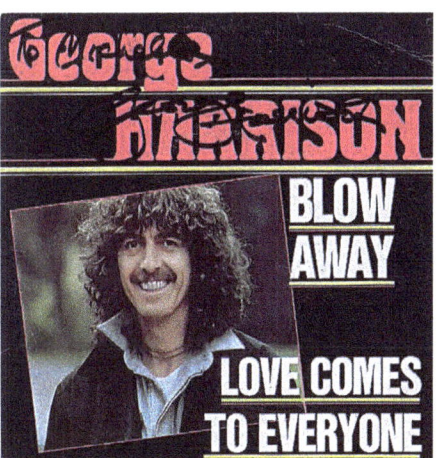

This picture sleeve for "Blow Away" and "Love Comes to Everyone" was signed in by George in 1979.

The Beatles Looking Back: The Final Trip

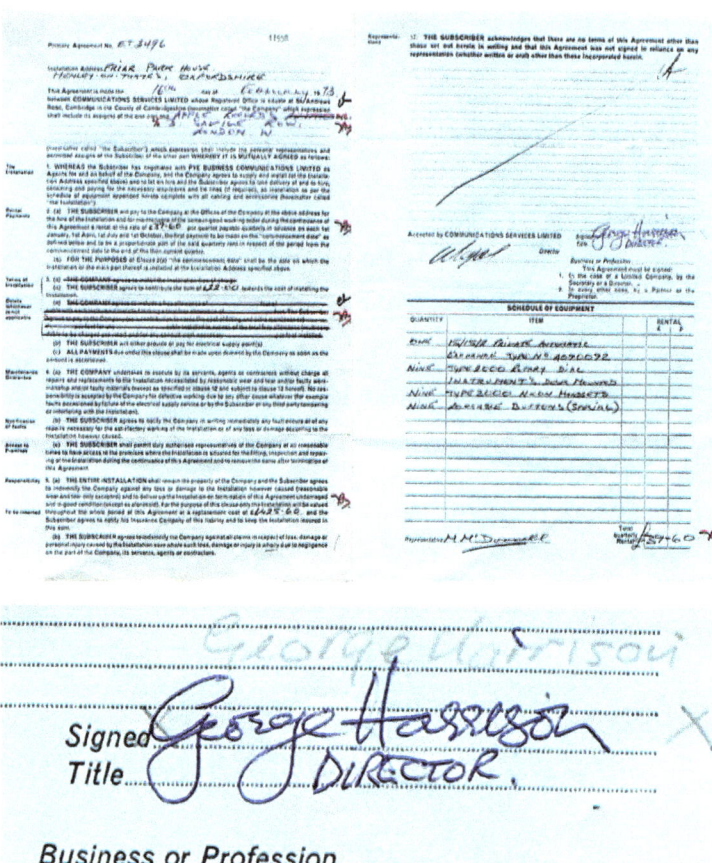

A hotel restaurant receipt with a imaginary name he used not most likely not to be disturbed but he did sign his name at the bottom. Seldom seen in this form

A two page contract with addresses Friar Park, Henley on the Thames (Harrison Residence) and Apple Reords on Saville Row, London in reference to Communications dated February 16, 1973 and signed by Harrison on the second page.

Below is a sampling of George Harrison's signatures obtained through the mail at the request of his fans.

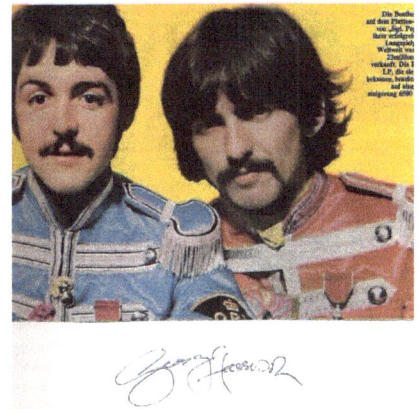

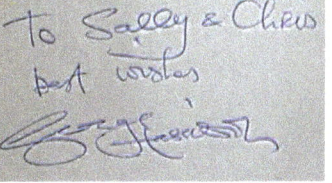

This signature above was obtained through the mail from a autograph request. George was hit and miss for signing mailed requests. If you sent a nice note with a self-addressed, stamped envelope you might have success, depending on what was going on in his personal and music life at the time. The other signatures on this page were obtained through the mail and in-person.

The Beatles Looking Back: The Final Trip

George was a big race fan and attended many races over the years. He released the single called "Faster" and he has signed nicely it the 45 picture sleeve.

George and others participated in and supported The Gun-ner Nilsson Cancer Treatment Campaign that was conducted January 6-13, 1979. George, an avid racing fan, and others have signed the program for the event. (Unfortunately, Gunner Nilsson had already lost his battle with cancer at age 29 on October 20, 1978.)

The Beatles Looking Back: The Final Trip

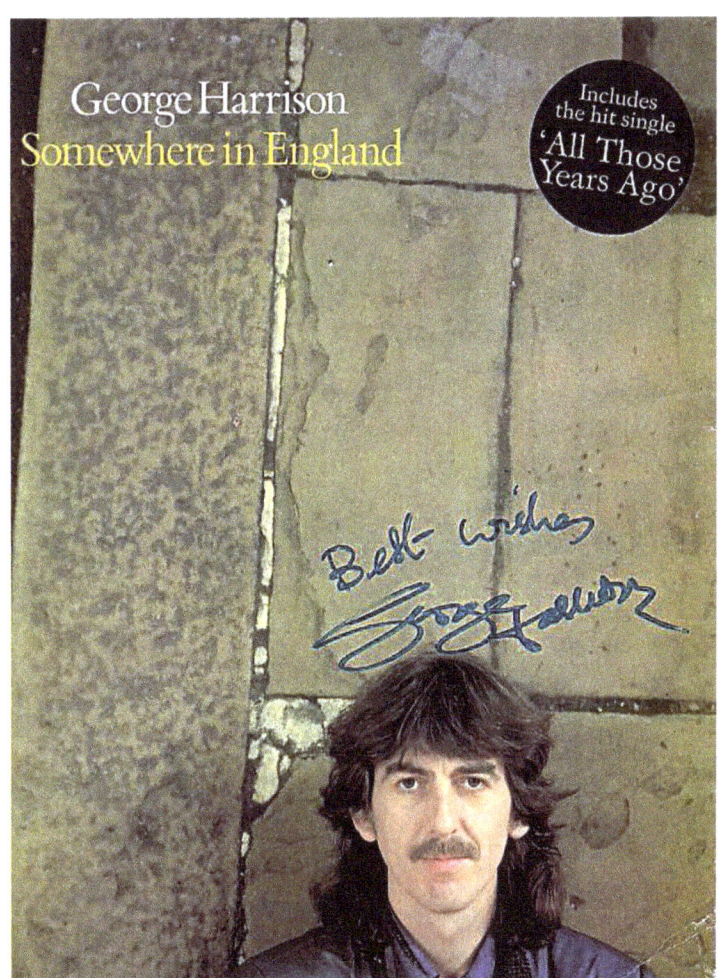

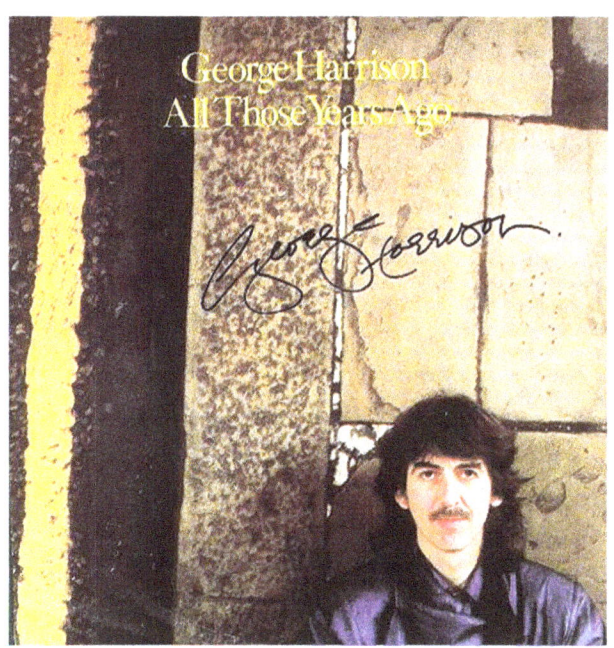

In 1981 George Harrison released his album Some-where in England, *featuring a tribute song to John Lennon called "All Those Years Ago." Here are two of those signed covers.*

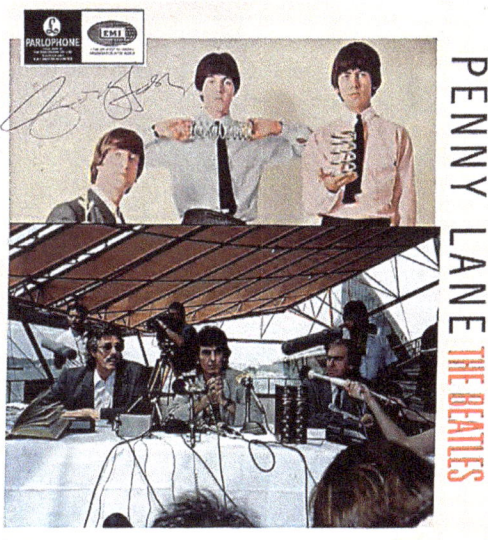

This UK 45 cover for The Beatles song "Penny Lane" was signed by George at a press conference in the 1980s.

GEORGE HARRISON SIGNED BEATLES ALBUMS

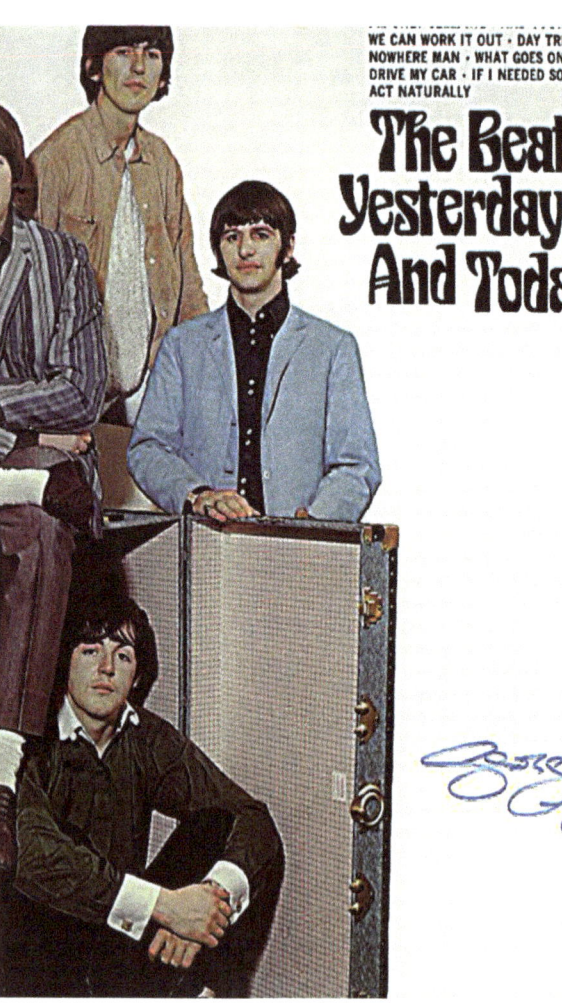

The Beatles Looking Back: The Final Trip

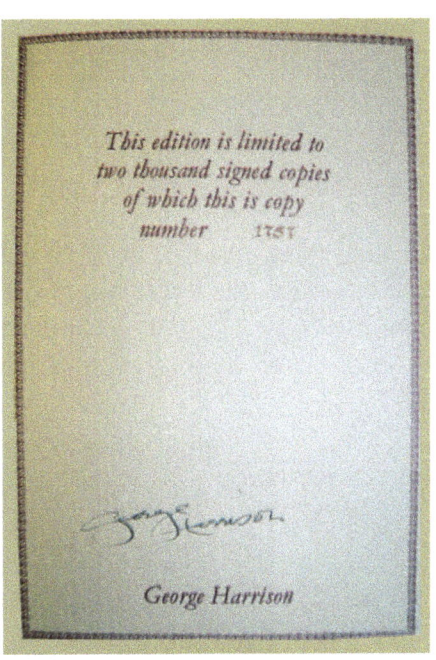

Genesis Publications limited signed edition of George Harrison's book, I Me Mine, *released in 1981, was signed by George and numbered 1757 of 2000 copies.*

In 1987, Genesis released three lithographs of artwork relating to George Harrison's songs "Taxman", "Piggies" and the most sought after one, "Here Comes the Sun", signed by George and artist Keith West.

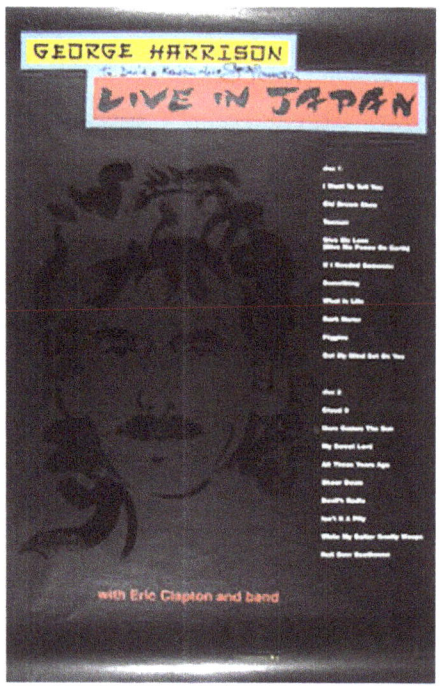

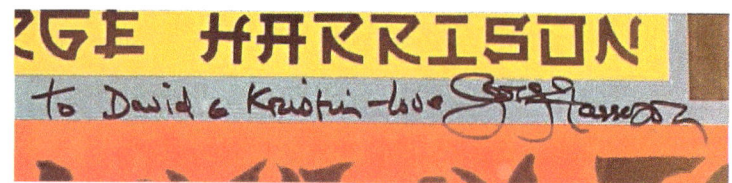

This promotional poster for George Harrison Live in Japan is signed and dedicated by George. This was George's second official live album release and was recorded during his joint tour of Japan with Eric Clapton in December 1991. The album was released in July 1992.

Nobody's Child: Romanian Angel Appeal was a charity album released in 1990 to benefit Romanian orphans, under the auspices of the Romanian Angel Appeal Foundation. Many artists donated songs. This album is signed by George Harrison and Ringo Starr.

George Harrison signature with OM symbol below on a Metropolitan Police Memo.

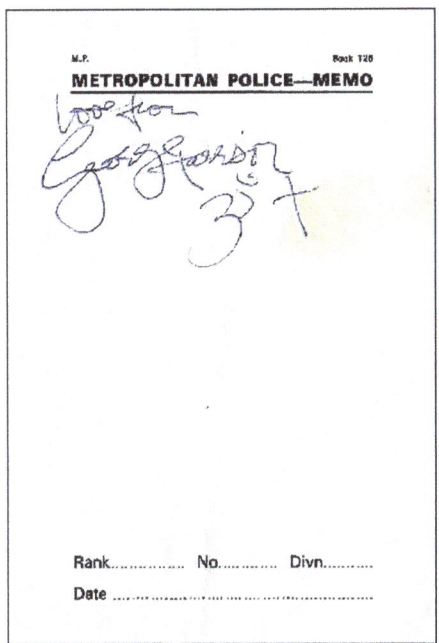

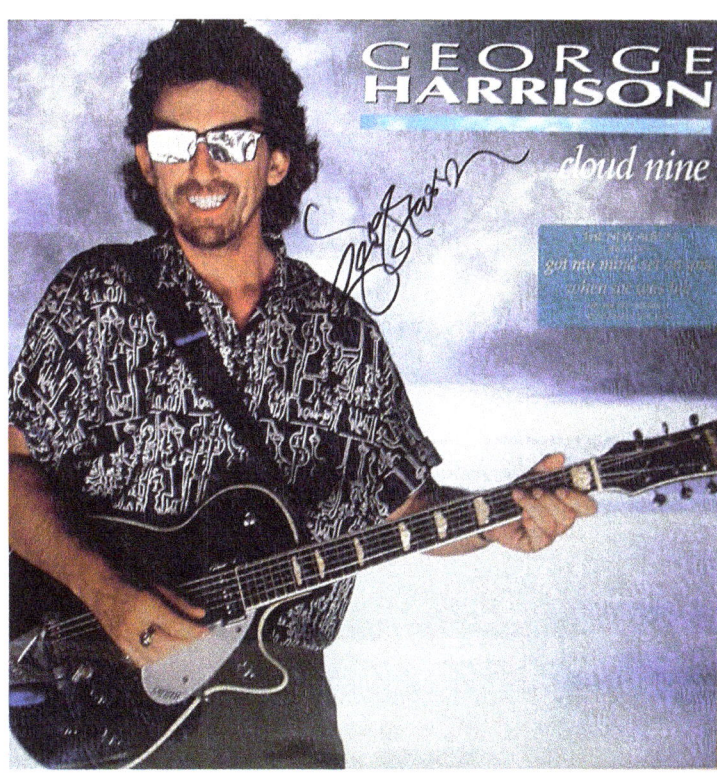

In 1987, George Harrison released the album Cloud Nine. *It garnered critical acclaim and featured many hit singles. This* Cloud Nine *cover has been signed by George.*

George Harrison signed this rare album proof for The Best of Dark Horse 1976-1989, *released in October 1989.*

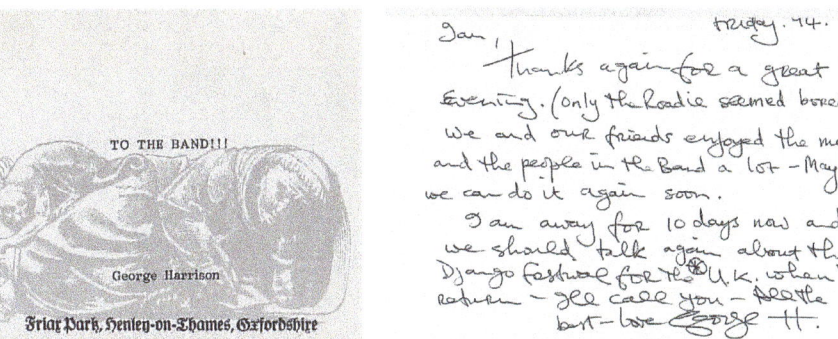

Handwritten George Harrison letter from 1994 from Friar Park in Henley.-on-Thames.

"The Beatles were just four guys that loved each other. That's all they'll ever be."

— Ringo Starr

(from *Beatles Anthology,* 2000)

Ringo Starr

"You know,
we can't go on forever as four clean little mop tops,
playing 'She Loves You.'"
— Ringo Starr
(to David Wigg, 1969)

The Beatles Looking Back: The Final Trip

Dear Carol
Thank you for the letter
I would be honoured to be your form mascot.
The only thing is what does a form mascot do
Sorry about writing the letter on the back of a photo but I have no paper
glad you like Boys.
Love Ringo Starr
xxx

A nice handwritten and signed note to a fan from 1963 by Ringo Starr. Signed on the back of a Beatles card.

The Beatles Looking Back: The Final Trip

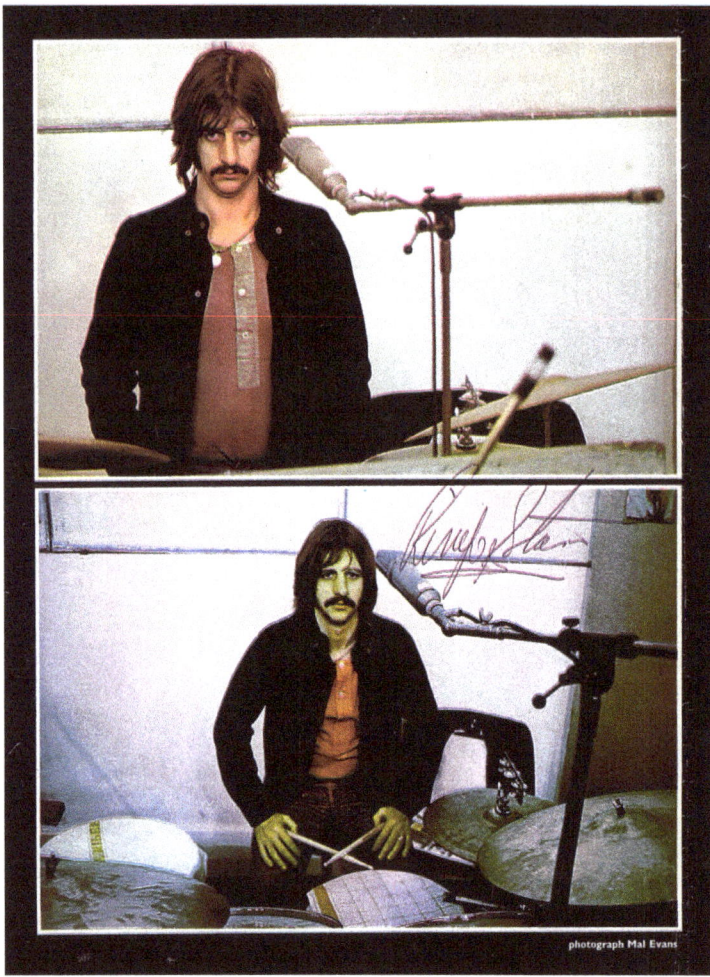

A photo page from The Beatles Get Back book signed by Ringo Starr to the right of his image in the 1970s.

The back of the UK pressing of the album With The Beatles, signed in 1964 by Ringo Starr.

Every now and then each Beatle would sign for the other three when they weren't present, as in this case with Ringo signing above.

This National Westminster Bank Limited check payable to British writer, Ray Connelly, was filled in by someone else and signed by R Starkey. Notice that Ringo added "Love" before he signed, which is quite rare on a check.

This District Bank Limited check dated September 10, 1970 and payable to Beatles & Co. is written in someone else's handwriting and signed by R Starkey, which is Ringo's real last name.

The Beatles Looking Back: The Final Trip

A program from a show Ringo attended in 1970 has been signed by him and Barry and Maurice Gibb, members of The Bee Gees.

A West Coast Premiere movie ticket for the movie *That'll Be The Day*, released in 1973, with Ringo co-starring with rocker David Essex. Ringo signed the ticket on the back.

A money/loan request TLS by Ringo to Wobble Music Ltd., signed R Starkey from 1975.

Ths Beatles 3rd series black and white trading card from 1964 was signed by Ringo Starr 20 years later after he received it in the mail as an autograph request. Scarce in this form.

The Ringo album signed on the cover by Ringo Starr

A lucky fan was at the right place at the right time, and obtained Ringo Starr's signature on the back of a boarding pass in the 1970s.

A nice Ringo Starr signature on a 3x5-inch, which he dated 86, on a 3x5 inch card.

The Beatles Looking Back: The Final Trip

The Beatles White Album *signed and dedicated by Ringo Starr on the front near the embossed title, along with the poster from the album, which was also signed by Ringo in the 1980s.*

A season's greetings card sent to Ringo's stepfather, Harry, signed by Ringo and wife, Barbara Bach.

A Shoney's restaurant menu signed on the front in the 1980s by Ringo Starr.

A handout photo card Ringo signed and sent in the mail to his fans who requested an autograph.

A 45 picture sleeve for the song "Wrack My Brain" from 1981, signed by Ringo and obtained through the mail.

A picture sleeve of "You're Sixteen," signed nicely by Ringo Starr. The signature was obtained during his 1989 All Starr Band tour.

A promotional 8x10 from the 1981 movie Caveman, signed by Ringo Starr.

A promotional 8x10 photo signed by Ringo Starr with his full name.

The Beatles Looking Back: The Final Trip

This Ringo Starr autographed Ludwig drumhead shows his full signature dated and is dated 92. Later that year, he stopped signing his full name, dropping his surname. Instead, he would sign Ringo and add a star drawing at the end.

Ringo Starr's full signature on this photo showing him on TV when he played Robin Valerian in Princess Daisy. The 1983 film co-starred his wife, Barbara Bach. His signature was obtained through the mail. Note, Ringo stopped siging his full signature in late 1992.

This black and white 8x10 photo of The Beatles, left, is signed on the front by Ringo Starr and George (Harrison). Ringo's signature was obtained through the mail, and George's was obtained in person.

The Beatles Looking Back: The Final Trip

Ringo Starr's full signature. What makes this interesting is that this signa-ture measured 10" wide on a 8 1/2 x 11 sheet of paper. Uncommon!

Pressbook for the 1972 movie Blindman, featuring Ringo Starr. Ringo signed this autograph due to a request through the mail. Ringo's first name signatures changed over the years but when he stopped signing his full name, he a added the drawing of a star.

The Beatles *Revolver* album cover signed on the front by Ringo Starr and his fellow band mate, George Harrison. Several attempts were made to get Paul to sign it fell short. However, since it left my hands, someone managed to secure Paul's signature on it.

The Beatles Looking Back: The Final Trip

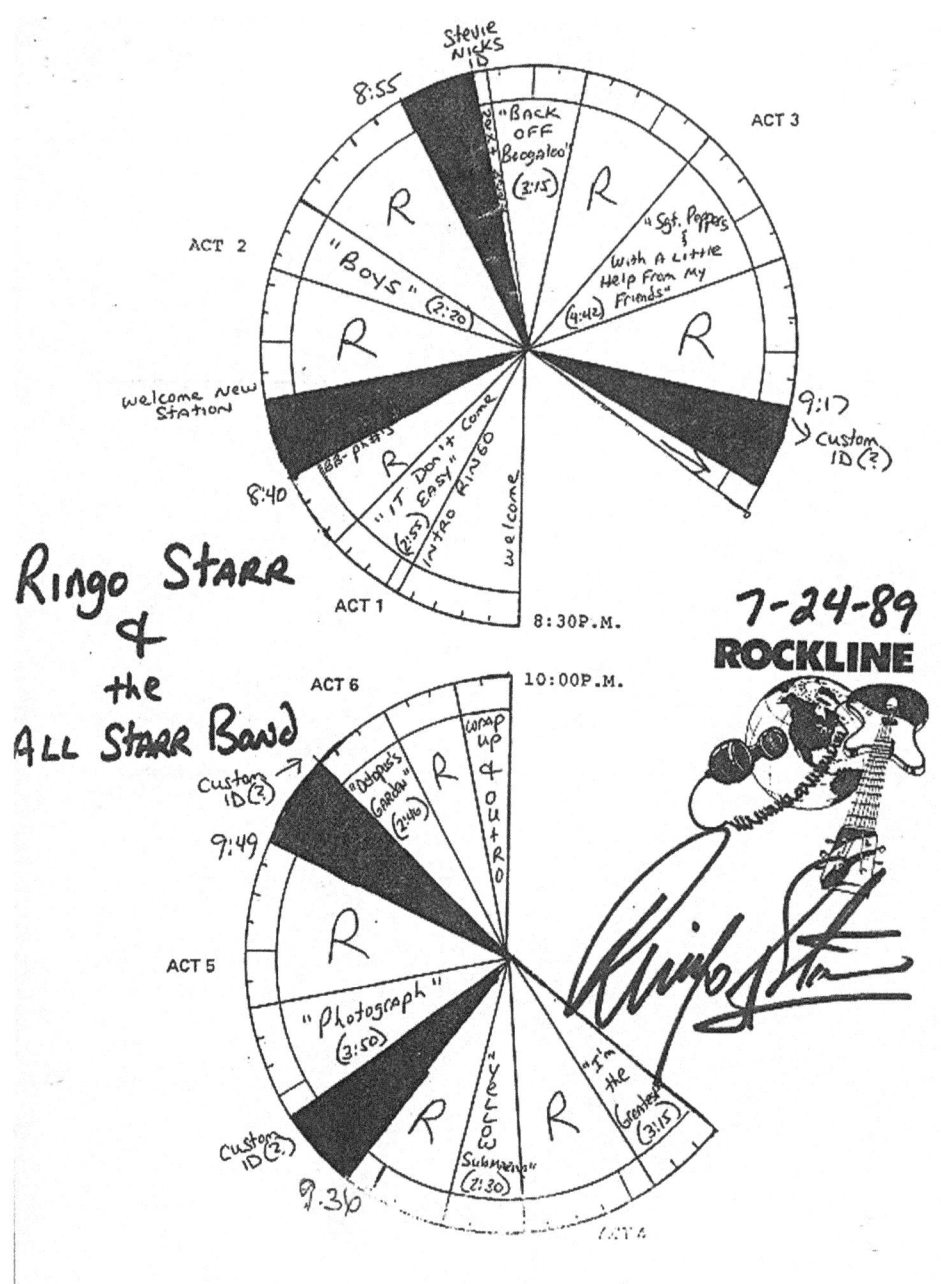

A Rockline time sheet for when Ringo appeared promoting his All Star Band Tour. He has signed the sheet and dated it July 24, 1989.

The Beatles Looking Back: The Final Trip

Dear George,

Happy Happy Birthday. Have a wonderful day and have one ppapaya on me.

Love,
Ringo xxx

A very rare fax from Ringo to George Harrison, wishing him a Happy Birthday in Hawaii.

A Ringo Starr and his All Starr Band tour program signed on the front by Ringo and other members of the All Starr Band along with actors Jack Nicholson, Gary Busey and musician Tom Petty, who attended the Los Angeles concert.

This nice photo of The Beatles, circa 1967, was signed by Ringo who also added a star.

Two drumheads signed by Ringo Starr. The first, large photo, was signed in 2003, and the second, small photo, was signed in the early 2000s.

The Beatles Yesterday and Today album cover was signed on the front by Ringo Starr in the 2000s.

Ringo Starr signed photos that were all obtained from requests sent through the mail.

The Beatles Looking Back: The Final Trip

RINGO STARR

Photo Credit: Cantanzaro & Mahdessian

The Beatles Looking Back: The Final Trip

This promotional jacket for Ringo Starr's All Starr Band Tour was signed nicely by Ringo with a large signature on the arm of the jacket by Ringo.

RINGO'S AUTOGRAPHS BY MAIL COMES TO AN END

On October 13, 2008, Ringo Starr, through a message on his website, asked fans not to send him any more mail at all. "No more fan mail and no objects to be signed. Nothing," he said. "Peace and love." Two days later, following backlash from fans, he further explained that his announcement was "in direct response to an inordinate amount of items which have recently appeared for sale on eBay." He was also concerned that all the correspondence amounted to "a waste of paper, and we all should be mindful of our carbon footprint." He finished by saying that if an item was postmarked before October 20, he would sign and return it.

I immediately started my letter to Ringo and enclosed a press conference photo of all four Beatles from the Indiana State Fair from when they appeared on September 3, 1964. I had been fortunate to get several items signed by Ringo through the years, and I knew this was my last opportunity. I also realized that because of all the last-minute requests he would likely be receiving it would be a long shot for me to receive anything from him. But, in his usual generous way, he did not disappoint and I did received the photo through the mail a couple of months later.

I met Ringo twice, and both times he was gracious enough to sign his autograph for me. The most memorable time was in July of 1989 when he, his wife Barbara, and the rest of the All Star Band arrived in Chicago from Dallas. It was his second concert with his All Starr Band. When the plane landed, several people exited, including members of the band. I waited, since I was there to meet Ringo. Once he came out of the plane, I approached him with some things I wanted him to sign and he politely told me, "Not right now."

I was disappointed, but something must have happened karmically because he stopped, turned around, looked at me and said, "Come, walk with us." The next thing I knew, I was walking through the airport with Ringo Starr, Barbara and their security guards. Ringo knew I was excited and even let me say those familier words that let me be that kid again: "I've been a fan of yours forever!"

As we exited the airport along with the rest of the band members, he stepped into the SUV limo waiting for him and looked at me once again. "Now give me everything you want me to sign," he said, and he did just that. This is one of my best memories and I'll never forget that encounter. I still think about it all the time.

Ringo Starr started signing things sent to him in the mail in the late 1970s, and even though it is disappointing that he stopped 2008, he truly was generous about it for all those years. All I can say as I finish is….

Thanks Ringo,
Peace and Love,
Tom Fontaine

Stuart Sutcliffe

"I looked up to Stu.
I depended on him to tell me the truth.
Stu would tell me if something was good
and I'd believe him."

— John Lennon

(said about Stuart Sutcliffe)

STUART SUTCLIFFE — THE FORGOTTEN BEATLE

Stuart Sutcliffe, who was born in Edinburgh, Scotland in 1940, grew up in Liverpool, England. He attended Liverpool Art College and was regarded as one of the best painters in his class, as well as a sketch artist and poet. It was here he met fellow classmate, John Lennon.

Sutcliffe helped Lennon improve his art skills and they became friends and roommates by early 1960. After talking to Sutcliffe one night at the Casbah Coffee Club, which was owned by Pete Best's mother, Lennon and McCartney persuaded Sutcliffe to buy a Höfner President 500/5 model bass guitar from Frank Hessey's Music Shop and become their band's bass guitarist. Sutcliffe's prior musical experience consisted of singing in the local church choir, piano lessons, playing bugle in the Air Training Corps, and learning some chords on the guitar from his father. While Stu could barely play, John wanted him in the band.

In September of 1960, while playing clubs day and night, Stu met photographer Astrid Kirchherr. They fell in love quickly and she became his fiancée two months into the relationship. While there, Astrid gave Stu a mop top haircut and the rest of the band soon followed which would later be known as The Beatle Haircut.

In May 1960, Sutcliffe joined Lennon, McCartney, and George Harrison (then known as "the Silver Beatles"). Sutcliffe's fingers would often blister during long rehearsals because he never practised long enough for his fingers to become calloused. He also started acting as booking agent for the band.

While the group performed in Hamburg, Germany, Sutcliffe's profile with the band grew after he began wearing Ray-Ban™ sunglasses and tight trousers, and his high spot was

singing "Love Me Tender", which drew more applause than the other Beatles, and increased the friction between him and McCartney.

Sutcliffe met Astrid Kirchherr in the Kaiserkeller Club while she was there watching the group perform. fter a photo session with the Beatles, Kirchherr invited them to her mother's house for tea. Sutcliffe began dating Kirchherr shortly after that. They were engaged in November of 1960 and Sutcliffe moved into the Kirchherr family's house.

On December 5, 1960, Harrison was sent back to Britain for being underage, and McCartney and Best were deported for attempted arson at the Bambi Kino. This left Lennon and Sutcliffe in Hamburg. Lennon eventually took a train home, but Sutcliffe had a cold he stayed in Hamburg. Sutcliffe later

borrowed money from his girlfriend, Astrid Kirchherr, so he could fly back to Liverpool on Friday, January 20, 1961. He eventually returned to Hamburg in March with the other Beatles.

Sutcliffe wanted to be with Astrid and continue painting, so in July of the same year, he decided to leave the group to continue painting.

While studying in Germany, Sutcliffe began experiencing severe headaches and acute light sensitivity, and some of the headaches left him temporarily blind. In February 1962, he collapsed during an art class, and Kirchherr's mother had German doctors examine him. The exact cause of his headaches could not be determined. The doctors suggested he return to the United Kingdom for further testing since they had better facilities.

He returned to the UK, but the doctors told him they could find nothing wrong, so he returned to Hamburg. He continued living with the Kirchherrs, but his condition worsened. He collapsed again on April 10, 1962. An ambulance was called and Kirchherr rode with him in the ambulance, but he died before they arrived.

Above, Stuart, John and George, signed by photographer Astrid Kirchherr. (Image from the Die Beatles in Hamburg postcard set.)

Right, Stuart Sutcliffe's handwritten poetry.

The cause of death was determined to be a brain haemorrhage, specifically a ruptured aneurysm that resulted in cerebral paralysis due to severe bleeding into the right ventricle of the brain. Sutcliffe was 21 years old.

On April 13, 1962, Kirchherr met remaining Beatles at Hamburg Airport and told them about Sutcliffe's death. Sutcliffe's mother flew to Hamburg with Beatles manager Brian Epstein and returned to Liverpool with her son's body. Sutcliffe's father didn't learn of his son's death until three weeks later because he was sailing to South America on a cruise ship. The family arranged for a military chaplain, to give him the news as soon as the ship docked in Buenos Aires.

The cause of Sutcliffe's aneurysm is unknown, although authors of books on The Beatles have speculated that it was caused by an earlier head injury obtained during an attack outside Lathom Hall after a performance in January 1961. According to booking agent Allan Williams, Lennon and Best went to Sutcliffe's aid, fighting off his attackers before dragging Sutcliffe to safety. Sutcliffe sustained a fractured skull in the fight and Lennon's little finger was broken. Sutcliffe refused medical attention and didn't show up for an X-ray appointment at Sefton General Hospital afterwards.

Stuart Sutcliffe influenced The Beatles in many ways, and it's sad that most people don't even know who he was in relation to the band's history. He was an incredibly talented artist, a gentle soul and Astrid's and John's best friend who left the world way too early.

Stu and John signed by photographer Jurgen Vollmer. (Image from the Die Beatles in Hamburg postcard set.)

The Beatles Looking Back: The Final Trip

This is an extremely rare handwritten envelope addressed by Stuart to his fiancée, Astrid Kircherr, in Hamburg, Germany. On the back he wrote: "From your Stuart". It is postmarked Liverpool, January 28, 1961.

Stuart Sutcliffe's personally owned and used book, Androcles and the Lion, with Stuart's signature on the front cover.

Both of these items came from the same poetry book owned by Stuart. It's interesting to note that he had at least two different styles of handwriting, as you see in these images. If you look carefully, he has also written his last name, Sutcliffe, over the cross-outs on the handwritten page on the right.

Stuart's personal book titled, From the Cape to Cairo, *with his signature on the inside cover.*

The Concert Years
(PRESS CREDENTIALS • ADVERTISEMETNS • TICKETS)

"When The Beatles arrived,
from then on,
a thousand different things arose."

— Pete Townsend

(The Who)

The Beatles Looking Back: The Final Trip

THE BEATLES AT THE HOLLYWOOD BOWL, LOS ANGELES, AUGUST 1964 & 1965

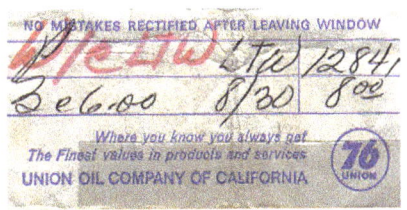

A pair of original concert ticket stubs, with envelope, from their appearance on August 30, 1965.

Original press credential pass dated August 23, 1964, with original invitation envelope from Hoopla Promotions, the company that sponsored the press conference.

Original ticket envelope postmarked April 1964, and concert ticket stub.

THE BEATLES IN CHICAGO, 1964 & 1965 AND BLOOMINGTON, MINNESOTA, 1965

This is an unused Beatle Battle Sales Contest order form with envelope from The Chicago Sun Times. *The winner of the contest got free tickets to The Beatles' appearance at the Ampitheatre on September 5, 1964.*

The Beatles handout program, 1964.

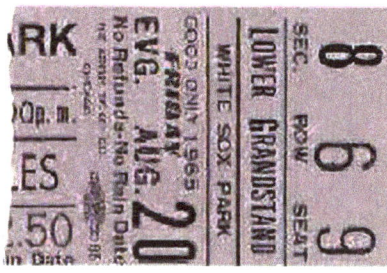

Original concert ticket stub from the concert at White Sox Park in 1965.

Original concert ticket stub from the Metropolitan Stadium concert in 1965.

THE BEATLES AT NEW YORK'S SHEA STADIUM, AUGUST 1965 & 1966

*Original 11x13-1/4" advertising proof with Sid Bernstein Enterprises stamp on the back *see inset) from 1965.*

Original concert ticket stub for The Beatles performance at Shea Stadium on August 23, 1966.

THE BEATLES IN HOUSTON, TEXAS, AUGUST 19, 1965

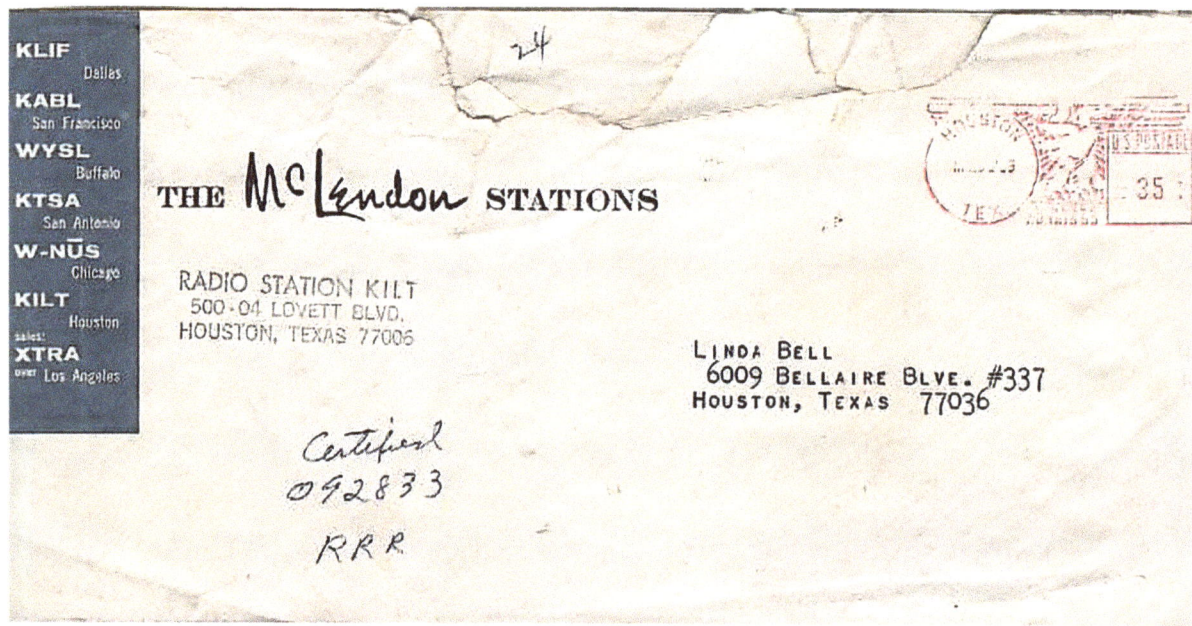

A pair of concert tickets for The Beatles performance at the Sam Houston Coliseum, with original envelope.

THE BEATLES IN PHILADELPHIA, PENNSYLVANIA, AUGUST 16, 1966

Very rare original Parking Permit Pass for the concert showing front, left, and back, right.

Original (rare version) of the concert ticket stub.

THE BEATLES AT DODGERS STADIUM, LOS ANGELES, AUGUST 28, 1966
AND CANDLESTICK PARK, SAN FRANCISCO, AUGUST 29, 1966
(THEIR LAST CONCERT)

Original concert ticket stub with envelope for the Dodgers Statium concert.

Two original concert ticket stubs from the Beatles last concert ever as The Beatles at Candlestick Park in San Francisco.

RARER THAN RARE

The extremely rare ticket stub for The Beatles' appearance at Rizal Memorial Football Stadium in Manila. Everything was normal about this appearance until the press accused The Beatles of snubbing the country's first lady, Imelda Marcos. This was never their intention, and they were more than happy to leave the country after their concerts. When the Beatles were later interviewed about this incident, you could tell they were not happy with the experience — especially John and George. Was this the straw that broke the camel's back regarding The Beatles touring other countries?

Original The Beatles press pass for their appearance at Convention Hall in Philadelphia on September 2, 1964. The pass was for someone from CBS and was signed by press officer Derek Taylor, which is rare. What makes this piece rarest of the rare is that it was also signed by all four Beatles at various times after the group disbanded in 1970. To date, this is the only press pass with all four signatures penned post Beatles. I must admit this was one of the items I wish I had kept.

"Everybody was influenced by somebody,
but I think everybody was influenced by The Beatles."
— Alice Cooper

INCREDIBLE!

Posters & Displays

"Sgt. Pepper's Lonely Hearts Club Band
is probably the greatest single album I ever heard.
The Beatles ultimately eclipsed a lot of what we'd worked for …
They eclipsed the whole music world."

— Brian Wilson

(the Beach Boys)

One-sheet movie poster for The Beatles' film A Hard Days Night *released through United Artists in 1964. It measures 27"x41".*

The Beatles' incredibly rare 6-sheet movie poster for Help! *Less then 300 of these posters were produced. The overall dimensions are 81"x81". They came folded as shown above, but unfolded it looks amazing!*

The Beatles original 1966 color (Butcher Cover) promotiomal poster for the album Yesterday and Today. This 18"x22" poster was released by Capital Records and featured the image of the Beatles in an avante garde way that did not settle well and was quickly deemed inappropriate. The image was quickly changed and stickers were made of that same image and pasted over the existing image to save having to print a new cover.

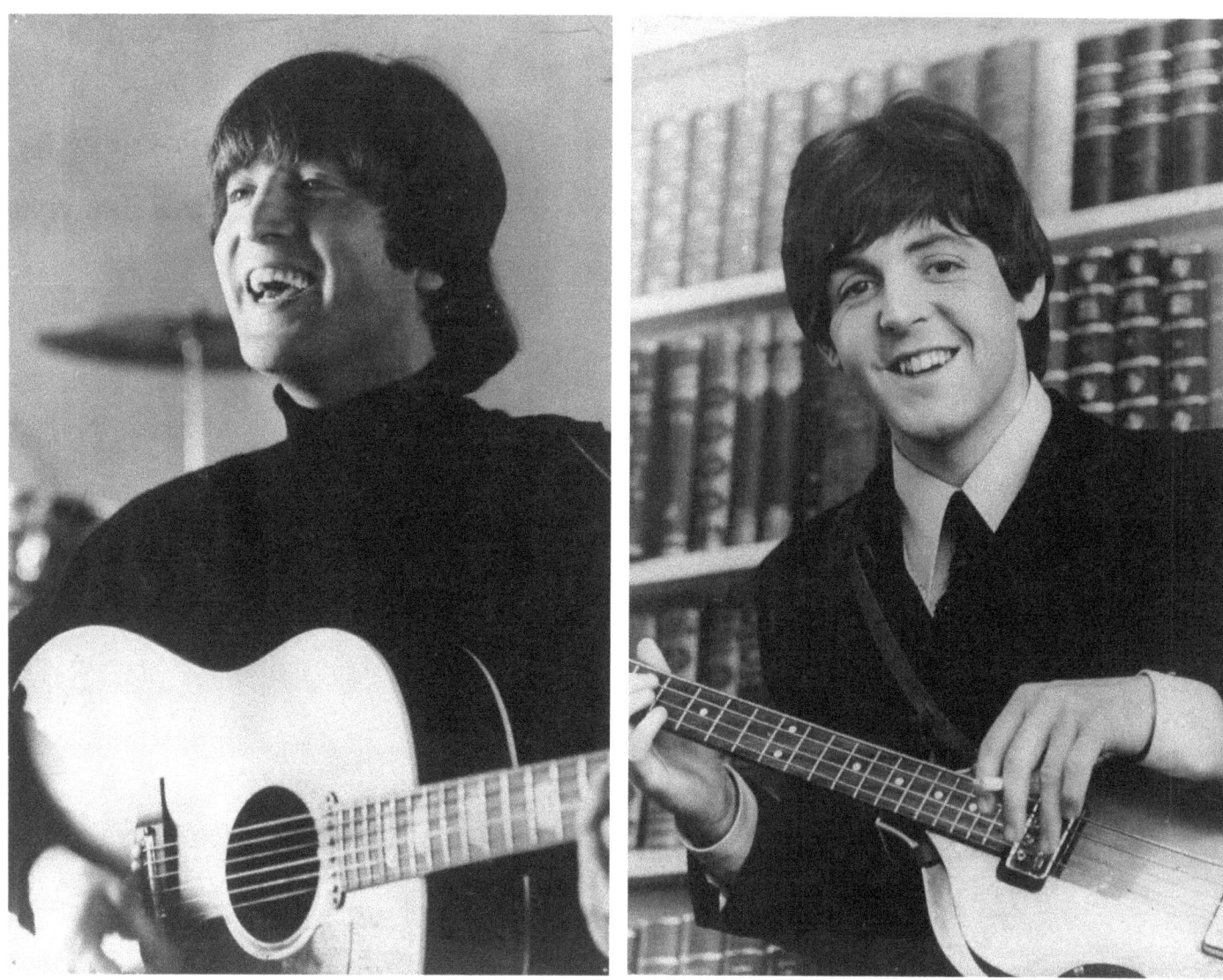

An extremely rare set of three 20"x30" posters on cardboard featuring John Lennon, Paul McCartney (above), and George Harrison and Ringo Starr (on the following page). According to my conversation with the recipient at time of purchase, these one-of-a-kind posters were made exclusively for a Help! *movie premier in the summer of 1965.*

The Beatles Looking Back: The Final Trip

The Beatles original 1965 window card for the movie Help! It measures 14"x22" card was used as an advertisement for the movie. United Artists sent these to a particular city and left the top blank so it could be filled in with specific information for that city. This particular one is for the Forest Theatre in Forest City, Iowa and tells the date and times for the shows.

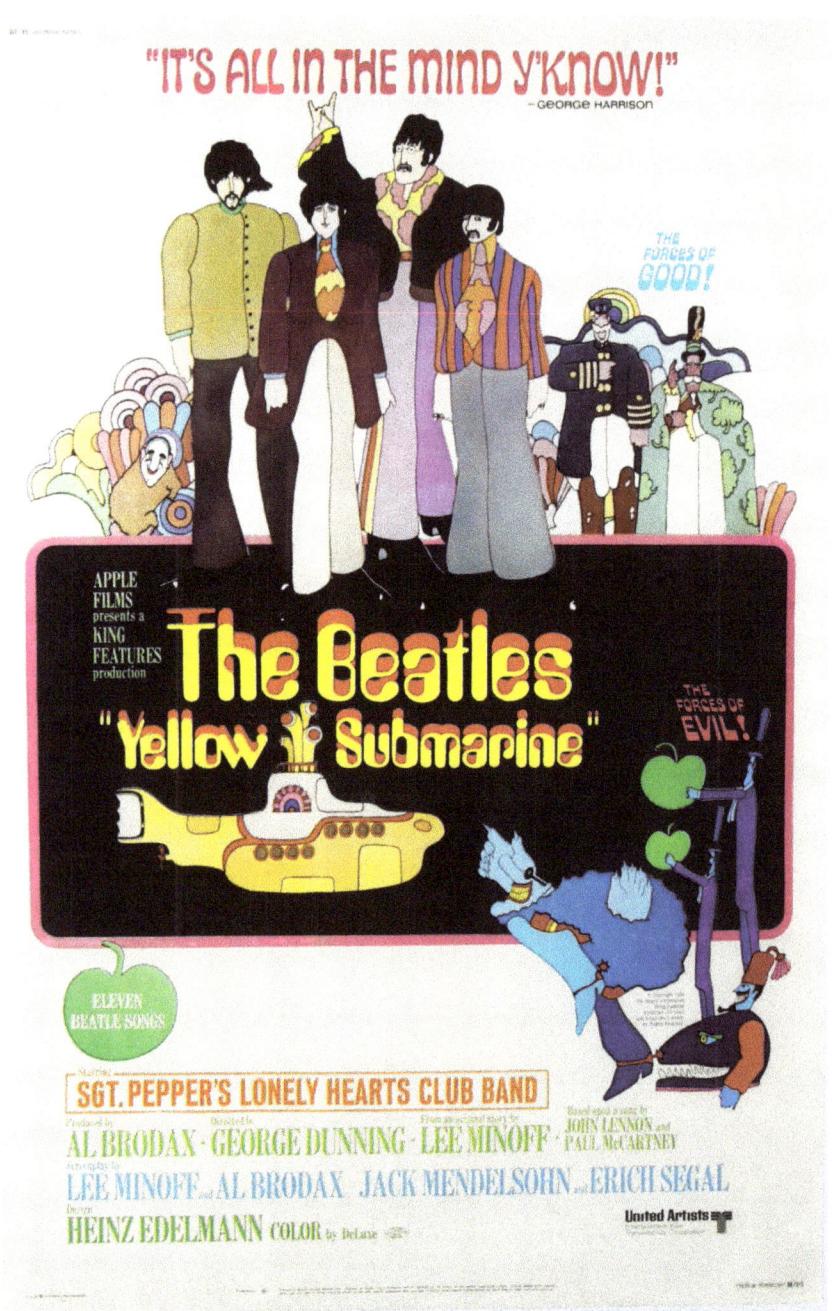

This original two-sheet subway poster for The Beatles' movie Yellow Submarine was printed and released in 1968. The poster features The Beatles in animated form, and measures 45"x59". The movie was released through United Artists. Rare in this form.

One-sheet movie poster for The Beatles' film, Yellow Submarine, released by United Artists in 1968. It measures 27"x41".

The Beatles Looking Back: The Final Trip

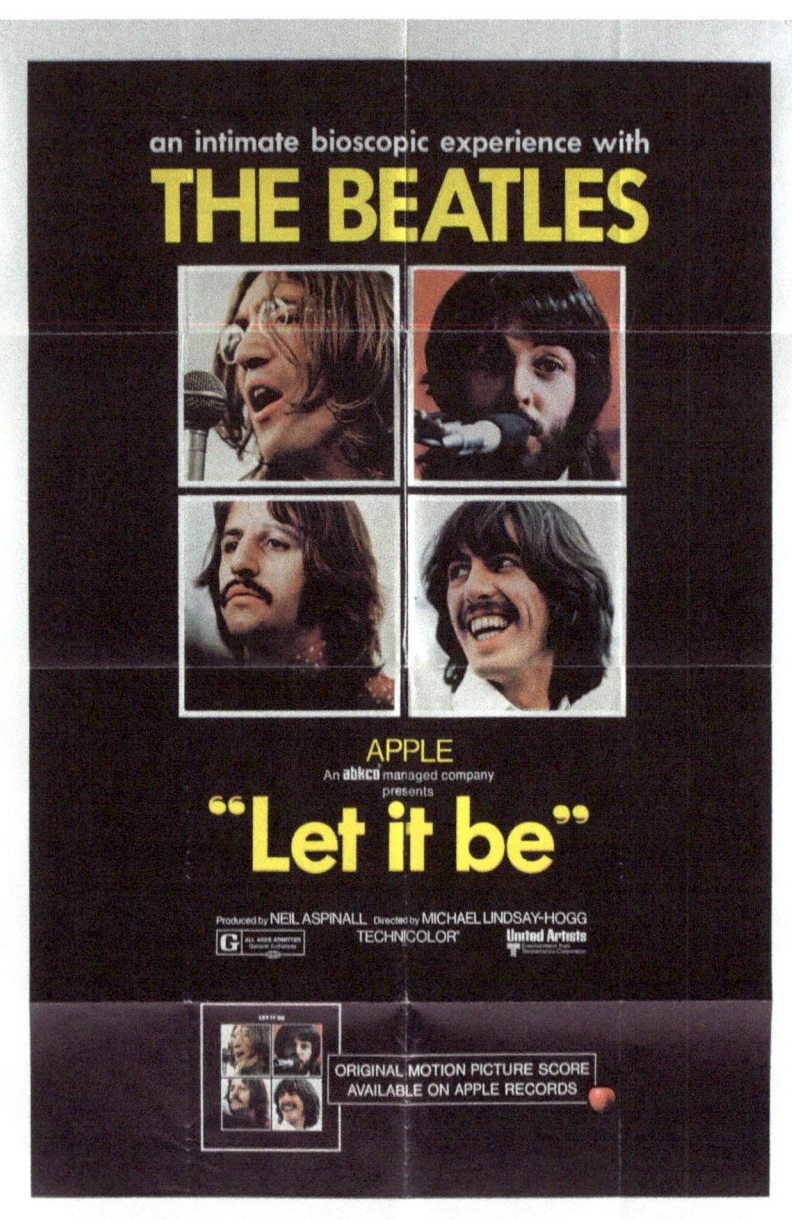

This is a one-sheet movie poster for The Beatles' film Let it be, *released by United Artists in 1970. It measures 27"x41". This was the last film The Beatles made as a group.*

This is a promotional poster for the re-release of The Beatles' masterpiece, Sgt. Pepper's Lonely Hearts Club Band. *It was released by Capital Records in 1982, and measures 20"x30".*

This was the Beatles' Help!/A Hard Days Night *home video display from MPI. It was used in video stores to advertise both films when they were released on VHS. In-store displays were hard to come by as a collector, because the store management would either return them to the company, or believe it or not, throw them away. This incredible and highly colorful display measures 40"x 70".*

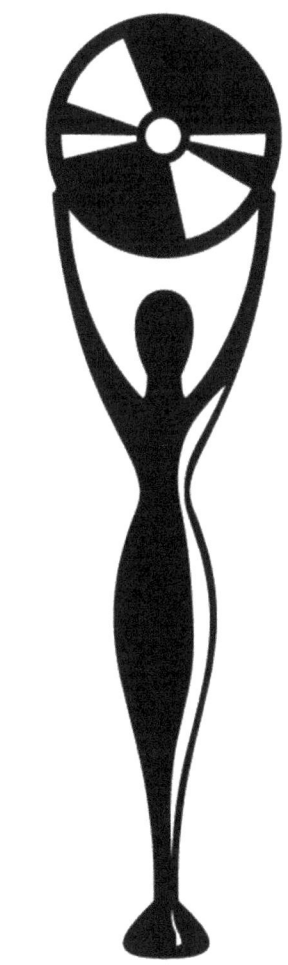

EPILOGUE
Rock 'n' Roll Hall of Fame

"I've been nominated to say hi and thank you.
You can sit down. I'm going to be here for hours....
I'd really like to thank everyone here
and everyone that's inducted us into the Hall of Fame...
Thank you, thank you, thank you."
— Ringo Starr
(at Rock 'n' Roll Hall of Fame induction of The Beatles)

"The reason we became a band is because of all of the other people who
are in the Hall of Fame already...
We just wanted to get guitars and get in a band
because we didn't have proper jobs at the time.
Anyway, it sort of turned out fine
and got a bit bigger than any of us expected."
— George Harrison
(at Rock 'n' Roll Hall of Fame induction of The Beatles)

FINALLY INDUCTED INTO THE ROCK 'N' ROLL HALL OF FAME

On January 20 1988 The Beatles were finally inducted into the Rock and Roll Hall of Fame. At that point, the band had split up 18 years prior in 1970, following the release of their 12th and final album Let It Be. The third annual event and took place at the Waldorf-Astoria Hotel in New York City.

The Class of '88 included The Beach Boys, The Supremes, and Bob Dylan, just to name a few. It was star-studded, who's who musical event. The George Harrison, Ringo Starr and members of the Lennon family accepted the award.

The following program contains the signatures of musicians, producers, etc. who attended the event.

This gentleman from New York was fortunate enough to meet and obtain several autographs on the inside of his program that evening; however, there was significant one missing. He was able to get Paul McCartney's signature at a later date, because he hadn't been at the event. He asked Paul to sign on The Beatles' photo page when he met him in New York.

As you look at all of the signatures in the image, see if you can figure out whose signatures he was lucky enough to get that night.

George Harrison speech the night of the event in his speech:

> "It's unfortunate Paul's the one who's not here because he's the one who had the speech in his pocket."
>
> "We all know why John can't be here, and I'm damn sure he would be," he added. "It's hard to stand here supposedly representing the Beatles. It's what's left I'm afraid. But we all loved him very much and we all love Paul very much."

ROCK AND ROLL HALL OF FAME

INTRODUCTION

WELCOME TO THE THIRD ANNUAL ROCK AND ROLL HALL OF FAME INDUCTION Dinner. To be eligible for induction this year, artists must have released recordings prior to January 1st, 1963.

From the start, rock and roll was a hybrid, if not a bastard form, and no one can dismiss the early importance of country and western music. Certainly, Elvis Presley's early Sun discs show the influence of C&W. Still, it remains incontestable that in its early years rock and roll was dominated by crossover artists from the R&B charts, including such previous inductees as Ray Charles, Fats Domino and Little Richard, and by white artists inspired by these performers.

The legacy of rhythm and blues continues to be honored this year, as the Hall of Fame inducts the Supremes and seven important members of the Drifters. One of Motown's flagship acts, the Supremes – Diana Ross, Mary Wilson and Florence Ballard – emerged during the height of the girl-group era. Their five consecutive Number One singles – "Where Did Our Love Go?" "Baby Love," "Come See About Me," "Stop! In the Name of Love" and "Back in My Arms Again" – hold the record in that genre.

The Drifters boasted an awesome succession of lead singers: Gerhart Thrasher, Bill Pinkney, Clyde McPhatter, Johnny Moore, Ben E. King, Rudy Lewis and Charlie Thomas. The group continued to have international best sellers for more than twenty years. What memories these hits conjure up: "Money Honey," "There Goes My Baby," "This Magic Moment," "Save the Last Dance for Me," "Up on the Roof," "On Broadway," "Under the Boardwalk" and the perennial "White Christmas."

The Beatles, the first of the British groups of the Sixties to be inducted, qualify this year because their first record, "Love Me Do," was released in the United Kingdom at the end of 1962, spearheading what has since been dubbed the British Invasion. In fact, rock and roll in Britain had begun in the late 1950s with artists like Tommy Steele, Cliff Richard and the Shadows and Johnny Kidd and the Pirates. But the Beatles not only helped to make Great Britain a permanent contender in the rock and roll sweepstakes but along the way changed the face of pop music forever. What started as an invasion might now be more appropriately called a twenty-five-year occupation. If anything, the British influence in rock and roll is growing stronger, and it has become common to see as many as seven British singles on the American Top Ten singles chart.

The music of John Lennon, Paul McCartney, George Harrison and Ringo Starr has enriched all of us. With their induction, we also honor their contemporaries – the Rolling Stones, the Who, the Animals, the Kinks, the Yardbirds – who will, without question, be considered for induction in the coming years.

The Beach Boys, who are the first white American vocal group to enter the Hall of Fame, released their first record, "Surfin'," in late 1961. For inspiration the Beach Boys drew upon the pop vocal groups of the late Forties and Fifties, most notably the Four Freshmen, stretching their melodic harmonies to fit rock and roll chords. Their music, however, at first mirrored the postwar California baby-boomer lifestyle, with songs like "Surfin' U.S.A.," "Fun, Fun, Fun" and "Little Deuce Coupe." As they matured, it became apparent that Brian Wilson, the group's leader, was a songwriter with an ability to combine classic pop melodies with unique chord progressions and lush harmonies never before heard in rock and roll. His genius, which influenced virtually every vocal group that followed, is perhaps most evident in songs like "Wouldn't It Be Nice" and "God Only Knows," from Pet Sounds, and "Heroes and Villains" and "Good Vibrations," from Smiley Smile.

To many in America, Bob Dylan's music stands as a symbol of the turbulence and unrest of the 1960s and the struggle for change that left its indelible stamp on that decade and the young people of a generation. His songs, like "The Times They Are A-Changin'," "Blowin' in the Wind," "It Ain't Me Babe," "All I Really Want to Do" and "Mr. Tambourine Man," touched on all the moral, social and political issues of the day. He is truly our first and perhaps greatest rock poet and was the most significant force in introducing and ensuring a permanent and rightful place for folk music in rock and roll.

It is fitting that in this same year we have also elected to induct as early influences two legendary folk artists who first made their mark during the Great Depression: Woody Guthrie, whose songs include "This Land Is Your Land," "Do Re Mi," "The Philadelphia Lawyer," "So Long, It's Been Good to Know You," and "Deportees," and Huddie "Leadbelly" Ledbetter, with compositions like "The Midnight Special," "Goodnight, Irene," "Boll Weevil," "Cotton Fields," "Rock Island Line" and "C.C. Rider." Both Guthrie and Leadbelly were an inspiration not only to Bob Dylan, the Byrds and others of their circle but to artists such as the Weavers, Cisco Houston, Ramblin' Jack Elliott, Sonny Terry and Brownie McGhee, Joan Baez and Peter, Paul and Mary, who kept the spirit of folk music alive and bridged the gap between the Dust Bowl ballads of the 1930s and the emergence of folk music in the early 1960s.

The third of tonight's inductees in the early-influence category is someone whose name is known to every kid who ever dreamed of becoming a guitar hero. Les Paul – who is perhaps best remembered today for his pioneering efforts in developing the electric guitar – was, together with his wife, the late Mary Ford, one of the top pop acts of the early 1950s. Although basically straight-ahead pop music, their revolutionary sound – combining multi-track electric guitars and voices on million sellers like "How High the Moon," "Vaya con Dios" and "Mocking Bird Hill" – was a major factor in helping to set new standards in recording excellence and technology.

Berry Gordy Jr., who is being honored tonight in the nonperformer category, first gained prominence as the songwriter of Jackie Wilson's early hits "Reet Petite" and "Lonely Teardrops" and later as both writer and producer of hits like "You Got What It Takes" and "I Love the Way You Love," by Marv Johnson. Gordy founded the Tamla label and the Motown Records Corporation in Detroit, in 1959, and remains the guiding light of the operation today. The continuous flow of hit records emanating from Motown – or "Hitsville, U.S.A.," as it was also called – was the single most significant factor in totally integrating rhythm and blues into the mainstream of pop music. In the previous decade labels like King, Specialty, Imperial and Vee-Jay had all made serious contributions to rhythm and blues. Chess was undoubtedly the greatest repository of blues music of that era, while Atlantic was able to emblazon the back of its singles sleeves with caricatures of its biggest acts and the slogan "Atlantic Leads the Field in Rhythm and Blues." But it was soon evident that Motown was more than an R&B label. Its slogan, "The Sound of Young America," was more than a boast; it was a reality to teenage record buyers, black and white, throughout the Sixties.

With so many great Sixties artists becoming eligible in the coming years for election to the Hall of Fame, there was concern that some of the important figures of early rock and roll might be forever overlooked. To guard against this, the nominating committee has decided to induct at least one nominee from the pre-Sixties era each year for the next ten years. With artists like Gene Vincent, Bobby "Blue" Bland, LaVern Baker, Duane Eddy, Dion, Bobby Darin, Hank Ballard, Lloyd Price and many other stars of that era still eligible, this decision was an absolute necessity.

In 1987, the Rock and Roll Hall of Fame building moved closer to becoming a reality, thanks to a great spirit of cooperation between our board and the Cleveland group, led by the governor of Ohio, Richard Celeste, the mayor of Cleveland, George Voinovitch, and Congresswoman Mary Rose Oakar. A Cleveland-based fund-raising committee has been established, with many of the leaders of that city's major corporations actively involved in the campaign. Most important of all, the world-renowned architect I.M. Pei has accepted our invitation to design and build the Museum, Library and Hall of Fame; a tentative site has been selected and a first-rendering scale model has been constructed. The building, as conceived by Mr. Pei and his staff, captures the vibrancy and excitement that typifies the music while retaining a dignity that befits the overall importance and endurance of rock and roll.

With deep sadness we note the passing of John Hammond, a founding board member of the Hall of Fame and an inductee in 1986. John Hammond's career spanned more than half this century, and he remained active in music until his death. At all times he was a true champion of new artists and emerging musical trends. He was always courageous and willing to take chances and always ahead of his time.

Finally, a spirited thanks to the companies and individuals who make up our board of directors, without whose tireless efforts and financial support the Hall of Fame could not exist.

Seymour Stein, *President*

INDUCTEES

INDUCTEES

www.ingramcontent.com/pod-product-compliance
Lightning Source LLC
Chambersburg PA
CBHW061348010526
44107CB00011B/872